Animal
Aviators

Masters of Flight

Animal
Aviators

Masters of Flight

By Eve Iversen

Franklin Watts
A Division of Scholastic Inc.
New York • Toronto • London • Auckland • Sydney
Mexico City • New Delhi • Hong Kong
Danbury, Connecticut

Interior layout by Jeff Loppacker

Photographs ©: Animals Animals: cover (butterfly), 3 bottom, 33 top, 34 bottom, 35 bottom, 36 bottom, 37 bottom, 112 bottom (Stephen Dalton), 11 (M. Deeble/Stone), 41 (Robert Maier), 97 (Peter Weimann); Archive Photos: 70 (Hirz), 78 (Reuters/Arcier), 25; BBC Natural History Unit: 56 (Jeff Foott), 76 top, 77 top (Tony Heald), 50 (Hans Christoph Kappel), 33 bottom (Duncan McEwan), 38 bottom, 39 bottom (Colin Varndell); Corbis-Bettmann: 8 (Christel Gerstenberg), 81 (Hulton-Deutsch Collection), 83 (Museum of Flight), 79 bottom (Leif Skoogfors), 85; Dembinsky Photo Assoc.: 40 (Claudia Adams), 29 (Stan Osolinski), 37 top, 73 (Rod Planck), 58 (Jim Roetzel), 38 top (Carl R. Sams); Liaison Agency, Inc.: 9, 68, 82 (Hulton Getty), 79 top (Philippe Poulet); Photo Researchers: 13, 34 top, 35 top, 49 (Stephen Dalton), 75 top (Gregory G. Dimijian), 43 (Francois Gohier), 61, 91 (Stephen J. Krasemann), 36 top (Frans Lanting), 32, 39 top (Tom & Pat Leeson), 63 (George D. Lepp), 74 top (Anthony Mercieca), 74 bottom, 75 bottom (Leonard Lee Rue III), 16 (Joe Tucciarone/SPL), 17 (Jim Zipp); Photri: 87; Superstock, Inc.: cover, chapter openers (seagull), cover (bat), 3 top, 67, 76 bottom, 77 bottom, 112 top; The Image Works: 80 bottom (M. Eascott), 80 top (Bob Mahoney); Visuals Unlimited: 53 (Jack Dermid).

Visit Franklin Watts on the Internet at:
http://publishing.grolier.com

Library of Congress Cataloging-in-Publication Data

Iversen, E. H. (Eve H.)
    Animal aviators: masters of flight / Eve Iversen.
        p. cm.
    Includes bibliographical references (p.)
    ISBN 0-531-11749-9
    1. Animal flight—Juvenile literature. [1. Animal flight. 2. Flight.] I. Title.
QP310.F5.I94 2001
573.7'98—dc21   00-036657

©2001 Franklin Watts, A Division Scholastic Inc.
All rights reserved. Published simultaneously in Canada.
Printed in the United States of America.
1 2 3 4 5 6 7 8 9 10 R 10 09 08 07 06 05 04 03 02 01

Contents

Introduction

The Dream of Flight

Did you ever wish you could fly? Humans have watched the flight of birds for thousands of years and envied their mastery of the skies. Numerous legends have told of humans, gods, goddesses, angels, demons, and spirits who were able to fly. Many people thought that all they needed to do was attach wings to their bodies.

The Greek myth of Daedalus and Icarus tells the story of a father and son who flew with wings they built. Daedalus, an architect, left Athens to work for King Minos of Crete. He built the Labyrinth, an underground maze so complex that anyone caught inside it was lost and trapped forever. The king had this frightful place constructed to hold the Minotaur, a monster with the body of a man and the head of a bull. Because the Minotaur would kill anyone he met, he had to be locked away.

7

This woodcut of the Daedalus-Icarus legend shows Icarus falling into the sea. After he flew too close to the sun, his wings melted.

Daedalus later fell out of favor with the king, who then imprisoned Daedalus and Icarus in a tower. In order to escape, Daedalus made wings from wax and feathers for himself and his son. Daedalus warned Icarus that if he flew too high, the heat from the sun would melt his wings. Once the two men were airborne, however, Icarus forgot this advice and flew as high as he could. The sun melted the wax in his wings, and he plunged to his death in the sea. The more cautious Daedalus landed safely.

Today, the name "Daedalus" stands for more conservative testing of new projects, while the name "Icarus" stands for testing the limits of an invention. People often use legends as symbols of ideas. The research journals *Icarus* and *Daedalus* symbolize two different approaches to aviation research—the study of human-engineered flight.

What is flight? Flight can be loosely defined as any deliberate activity that permits an animal or a person to leave the Earth's surface and maintain control over their return to Earth. Why might an animal or a person want to fly? To get away from a *predator* perhaps, to get food, or to travel by the shortest route. People often use the expression "as the crow flies" to describe the most direct route between two points.

Humans have always wanted to fly, and they eventually learned by watching animals such as birds, bats, and insects. These true fliers can control their flight and increase their *altitude* at will. This ability marks the difference between true fliers and mere gliders. By studying the principles of flight, or *aerodynamics,* in animals, people gained the knowledge that makes modern air travel possible.

It is humbling to realize that it was only about a century ago that Orville Wright flew the first heavier-than-air aircraft, while nature's aviators have been traversing the skies for millions of years. It took centuries for humans to even begin to understand why animals are such successful fliers.

In 1909, six years after Wilbur and Orville Wright made their famous flight in the United States, Wilbur demonstrated his airplane in France.

Unpowered Flight: Gliding and Soaring

Wings aren't necessary for *unpowered* flight. A variety of animals who don't have wings can take to the air. Young spiders, or spiderlings, produce a silk parachute that allows them to catch a breeze and "float" through the air for hours in search of a new home. Some fish, amphibians, and reptiles can stay aloft for varying periods, as you will learn in this chapter. Several kinds of mammals can glide, but only bats can fly under their own power.

Gliding, which may have been the first form of airborne movement developed by animals, involves moving from one place to another through the air by controlled descent. The downward pull of gravity cannot be overcome though, so once the animal takes off, the only path is down. Gliding often involves the use of a skin flap or other body part that allows an animal to jump from a height and steer toward its destination, whether the surface of the water, a tree branch, or a patch of ground.

Flying Fish

Have you ever seen a fish glide through the air—above the surface of the water? Some fish use their ability to "fly" to escape their enemies, but sometimes their efforts land them on the decks of ships. In a report of the 1947 voyage of the raft *Kon-Tiki* across the Pacific Ocean, the Norwegian explorer Thor Heyerdahl wrote that his crew used stranded flying fish for breakfast. According to Heyerdahl, "It sometimes happened that we heard an outburst of strong language from a man on deck when a cold flying fish came unexpectedly, at a good speed, slap into his face."[1]

In a flying fish, the tail provides the propulsion that allows the fish to be about 36 inches (91 cm) above the surface of the water for up to 328 feet (100 m)—about the length of a football field. A flying fish that jumps out of the water to escape predators can glide through the air for a few minutes. While still under water, the fish builds up speed with its fins held close to its body. When the fish breaks the surface, it spreads its fins, and its tail gives it extra propulsion. Once the fish is flying, it pulls up its tail.

A flying fish uses its "wings," which are actually modified fins, to glide above the water and escape predators.

Fish that have the ability to "fly" live in saltwater and freshwater. About 40 species of silvery ocean-dwelling fish have rigid, winglike fins that are used in flight. Others such as the California flying fish, the largest of all flying fish, have both pectoral (side) and pelvic (leg) fins modified into wings. Nine species of freshwater hatchetfish fly by flapping their pectoral fins. The two "wings" of some species are actually modified pectoral fins.

Gliding Frogs and Reptiles

Frogs, which are amphibians, undergo metamorphosis—that is, they begin life in freshwater and develop into creatures with lungs and legs that are adapted for life on land. Most of these creatures move by swimming or hopping, and some are among the world's best leapers. But sometimes they need to take to the air in another way—perhaps to get away from predators. One group of remarkable tree-dwelling frogs in Asia (genus *Rhacophorus*) moves by gliding. To control their fall, the frogs have webs that extend between their toes on all four feet. By extending these webs, the frogs can glide from one tree to another.

Can snakes "fly"? One kind of snake (genus *Chrysopelea*) that lives in Malaysia can make controlled descents from one tree to another. When the snake takes off, it spreads its rib cage so that its body is flattened and the bottom surface is curved downward as much as possible. This increases the air resistance on its body and decreases its rate of fall. The snake can glide for about 98 feet (30 m), and it can even change direction while descending. After it lands on another branch, it continues to hunt. The gliding snake is not poisonous.

Most lizards move by crawling. In the forests in Southeast Asia, you might see one hunting for insects at the base of a tree. It then climbs up the tree and continues its search. To get to another tree, it glides on its "wings"—formed from five or six extended ribs covered by flaps of skin. This lizard belongs to the genus *Draco,* but some people call it the "flying dragon" because of its ability to travel through the air. When this lizard is not "flying," it folds its "wings" against its body. When it wants to begin hunting for food, it launches itself to the base of another tree using its "wings" to help glide and its tail to help steer.

Gliding Mammals

Bats are true fliers with well-developed wings, but other mammals have also developed the ability to "fly." They live in trees in many parts of the world, and their ability to glide through the air is a great advantage.

Flying squirrels are mammals who use their ability to glide to avoid predators or travel through a forest without crossing the ground. To glide from one tree to another, the squirrels use the flap of fur-covered skin that runs along the sides of their bodies between the front legs and the back legs. To steer, they use their tails. They lose altitude when they fall, but they travel three times as far horizontally as they fall vertically. For instance, a flying squirrel that takes off and glides for 30 feet (9 m) ends up 10 feet (3 m) lower than where it started.

Flying squirrels live in North America, Europe, Asia, and Africa. In all flying squirrels, the membranelike skin flaps are strengthened by cartilage— the same strong yet flexible tissue you have in your nose. In the North American and Eurasian squirrels, the flaps are attached at the wrists. But in the squirrellike rodents who live in Africa, the flaps are attached to the elbows.

A flying squirrel glides from one tree to another using skin flaps to control its descent.

Flying squirrels of the genus *Glaucomys* live in the United States, but it is difficult to see them in the wild, because they are nocturnal animals—active at night. They live in colonies and may even build their nests in birdhouses.

Phalangers are the marsupial equivalent of flying squirrels. Marsupials are mammals with a pouch used to protect the newborn young, who are not fully developed when they are born. Phalangers live in New Guinea, Australia, and Tasmania. Like flying squirrels, the so-called flying phalangers are tree-dwelling animals who glide from tree to tree in open forests. To sail through the air, most of them use the furry flaps that run along their sides. To steer, they use their tails. Flying phalangers don't land gently—they actually bounce!

Another interesting gliding mammal is the colugo. This creature, sometimes called a "flying lemur," lives in Southeast Asia, Malaysia, and the Philippines and is not related to the lemur of Madagascar. Like phalangers and flying squirrels, colugos use skin flaps to glide from tree to tree. But they also have skin flaps that stretch between the throat and the front legs and between the back legs and the tail. With this extensive surface area, they have more air resistance and a smaller rate of fall than phalangers. Malaysian colugos can glide for over 279 feet (85 m).

Prehistoric Animal Gliders

The ability to glide is not limited to the animals we know today. Scientists are continuing to discover *fossils* and find more examples of ancient creatures that took to the air. It turns out that flying fish are not the only animals who lived in the oceans who have the ability to glide. Research on fossil sharks has led some scientists to believe that at least one of these animals could "fly." It had the same type of modified pectoral fins as saltwater flying fish. This shark may have used its ability to become airborne to escape larger predators.

Scientists have also discovered fossil reptiles that could glide. None of these flying reptiles is a dinosaur or directly related to birds. Some of these animals may have been able to fly the same way birds do (see Chapter 3).

An ancient reptile that scientists call *Sharovipteryx* (formerly known as *Podopteryx*) was definitely a glider. It lived in places such as central Asia during the Triassic Period (about 225 to 190 million years ago). *Sharovipteryx* may have moved much as flying squirrels do. About the size of a mouse, it had one skin flap that stretched from its arms to its legs and another that stretched from its legs to the middle of its tail.

In the 1990s, Russian researchers found the fossilized bones of a reptile named *Longisquama*. This fossil of an animal is believed to have lived in the early Triassic Period (about 220 million years ago) on the ancient supercontinent Pangaea, and its appearance has sparked a lively debate.

These sparrow-sized animals had featherlike structures growing from their backs. Scientists are not sure whether these were used to help control a fall or were part of a "threat" display. If these structures were brightly colored, the reptiles may have raised or lowered them to make themselves appear larger to a rival or more attractive to a member of the opposite sex. In any case, *Longisquama* is one of the most unusual reptiles in the *fossil record*.

During the late Triassic Period (about 190 to 180 million years ago), gliding reptiles called *Icarosaurus* lived in what is now New Jersey. These animals had elongated ribs that supported a skin flap divided into two parts. *Icarosaurus* may have used these "wings" to glide from tree to tree the way "flying dragons" do today. Other reptiles with skin flaps may have moved through the air in the same way.

Of all the prehistoric flying reptiles, the *pterosaurs* are probably the best known. These creatures, which have been known for nearly two centuries, evolved from ancient walking reptiles around the time of the dinosaurs. Pterosaurs, such as *Pteranodon*, often appear in books and paintings of animals of the Mesozoic Era (230 to 65 million years ago). Pterosaurs also shared the skies of the late Mesozoic with early birds.

All of the many pterosaur species had long, narrow wings, which evolved from the fourth finger of the reptilian hand. The wings were made up of elongated bones and skin and were attached to the body in different places in each species.

The more primitive pterosaurs lived in the Jurassic Period (about 190 to 140 million years ago). They usually had a full set of teeth, a short neck, and a pronounced tail. The more advanced pterosaurs lived in the late Jurassic and early Cretaceous Periods (about 140 to 130 million years ago). Their teeth were fewer and smaller, and some animals were even toothless. They also had a long neck and a short tail.

The pterosaurs ranged in size from that of a sparrow to a bird much larger than one of the largest birds living today, the Andean condor, which weighs 20 to 25 pounds (9 to 11.25 kg) and has a wingspan of 10 feet (3 m). Large pterosaurs, such as *Pteranodon*, which weighed 37 pounds (17 kg), had a wingspan of about 21 feet (7 m). These larger animals may have spent most of their time *soaring,* just as condors do today.

The massive *Quetzalcoatlus,* which may have weighed 143 pounds (65 kg), had a wingspan of more than 49.2 feet (15 m). Fossils of *Quetzalcoatlus* have been found in Texas. When scientists first estimated the size of *Quetzalcoatlus,* many people made jokes about the size of the

The pterosaur Quetzalcoatlus, *which was named after a feathered serpent god worshipped by people in ancient Mexico, is the largest flying reptile known to scientists.*

animal—it seemed to be fit for the vast skies of Texas. *Quetzalcoatlus* has been the subject of much debate. Did it actually fly, or did it just glide?

Scientists are trying to determine which pterosaurs were gliders and which were true fliers. Pterosaurs had many features in common with modern birds, and so some researchers have concluded that many species were active fliers. Like birds, pterosaurs had a large *keel-shaped* breastbone that allowed for the attachment of the large flight muscles. They also had a chest and "arm" that were similar to those of birds.

The wing structure of pterosaurs was not like that of birds, however. Pterosaurs had wings made of skin supported by an elongated fourth finger, much like bats. In contrast, birds have feathered wings with no bony supports. (See Chapters 3 and 4 for more information.) Pterosaurs had cartilage to support their wings, while bats use bone. Pterosaurs also had relatively narrow wings that were attached to their body rather than their feet, like bats wings.

Soaring Birds and Butterflies

If you're ever in a valley on a warm afternoon, look up high in the sky, and you may see birds with their wings outstretched, moving in circles over cliffs. They are engaged in another kind of unpowered flight—soaring, a kind of gliding that involves the use of true wings.

These large birds are taking advantage of something that causes the "bumpy" ride in an plane—columns of warm air rising from the ground. As air is heated by the sun, it becomes less dense and rises in vertical currents called updrafts. Birds and other fliers, such as humans in gliders, may obtain lift while soaring on these thermals.

The columns of warm air are associated with forests, rocky terrain, and other surfaces that absorb more heat than nearby areas. So animals who soar have the ability to rise through the air, even without using their wings. Sometimes they can cover vast distances without having to expend the energy needed for flapping.

Soaring is often associated with birds of prey, such as hawks, eagles, vultures, and condors. Other birds, such as the albatross, and insects, such as the monarch butterfly, who migrate for long distances, are able to use updrafts to ascend and can stay aloft with minimum effort. "Riding" the thermals isn't only for large birds.

A red-tailed hawk, a fairly common bird of prey in the United States, often soars by using its broad wings to "ride" the thermals.

Chapter 2

Powered Flight: The Desire for More Control

An animal that glides does not have complete control of its flight path—for one thing, it cannot gain altitude. By contrast, watch a pigeon in flight. It can move in any direction, even backward, and it can go up or down. It has control over its flight path.

Powered flight describes heavier-than-air flight in birds and humans. To take off, birds need a lot of energy. How do they overcome gravity and lift themselves off the ground? They use their own muscles to supply the necessary power. Airplanes use power from internal combustion engines (like those in automobiles) or jet engines. By studying true fliers such as birds, scientists have gained a better understanding of how animals fly, and they have applied it to human-engineered flight. The basic principles that apply to animal flight are used to build and operate aircraft.

All That Air

All wings, whether they're on birds, bats, or airplanes, are designed to move through the air, which is a mixture of gases. However, air is also a fluid, because it is composed of particles that move easily and change position quickly. The air itself has weight because it has mass and is subject to the pull of the Earth's gravity. An object weighs less when gravity is reduced, even though the object has not changed in any other way. This is why astronauts "float" in space where there is little gravity.

Because air is a gas, it can easily expand when heated and contract when cooled. The *density* of air can vary. More compressed air is more dense, and cool air is more dense than warm air. Air closer to the Earth's surface is both heavier and more dense than air at higher altitudes because of the *pressure* of the air above it. Atmospheric pressure is the force that the total air in an imaginary column exerts on a given surface area. The air above your head, which is held there by the Earth's gravity, extends upward for hundreds of miles. The closer you are to the Earth's surface, the more the air column presses on you.

Flying Fundamentals
Airfoils and Wings

Wings, whether they're on birds, bats, insects, or airplanes, have the same basic structure and are designed to function the same way. They all move in air, which is a fluid. A Swiss mathematician named Daniel Bernoulli was interested in increasing the speed of ships by making their movement through water, another fluid, as effective as possible. In 1735, Bernoulli shared a prize from the Paris Academy of Sciences with his father, who also did scientific work. The older man was once so jealous of his son that he threw him out of the house for investigating the same topic.

Bernoulli later determined the relationship between pressure, density, and *velocity*. He found that the greater the velocity of a fluid, the less pressure it exerts. In other words, fast-moving air exerts less pressure than slow-moving air. People later applied this idea, known as *Bernoulli's principle,* to the design of aircraft wings.

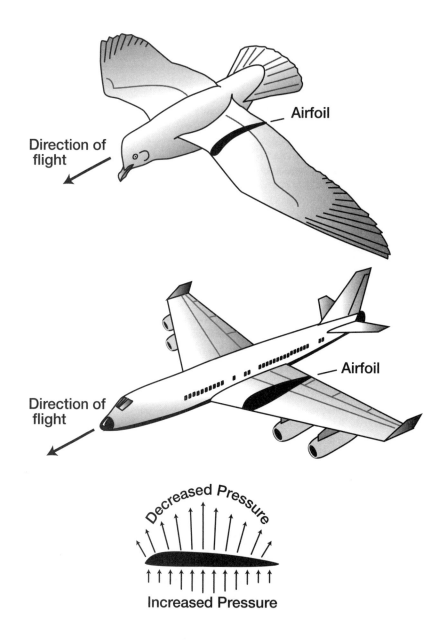

Both birds and airplanes have wings that are curved in cross-section—they are airfoils. Bernoulli's principle states that the greater the speed of a fluid, such as air, the less pressure it generates. As birds and airplanes fly, the air moving along the curved upper surface has to travel faster to meet the air moving along the lower surface. The greater pressure under the wing pushes it up.

Bernoulli's Principle

Two simple experiments demonstrate Bernoulli's principle.

1. Cut a piece of paper 4 inches long by 1 inch wide (10 cm by 2.5 cm). Put it in a book like a bookmark, with part of it sticking out. Blow across the paper while keeping the book shut. Watch how the paper reacts to the wind traveling above and under its surface. What should happen? What does happen?

2. Put a Ping-Pong ball on a table and cover it with a funnel. Blow into the funnel steadily while allowing the air to escape from under the funnel. Don't hold the funnel down. The high-speed air coming out of the funnel creates an area of low pressure above the ball. The air below the ball is at a higher pressure. What should happen? What does happen?

Have you ever traveled in a car on a day when there is no breeze? When you put your hand out the window you could feel the force of the wind even though there was no wind outside. Your hand was feeling the relative wind caused by the car's moving through the air. If the car traveled fast enough, you may have felt your hand lift up as the speed over the top of your hand created lift under your palm. That's Bernoulli's principle at work.

A bird's wing is a good example of an *airfoil* and also illustrates how Bernoulli's principle works. As the bird flies, the air flows over the wing surface, and it splits into two streams. Both pass over the front edge of the wing and move to the back edge. One stream passes over the top of the wing. Because the wing is curved, with more surface area on top, the air has farther to travel. To meet the air passing over the lower surface, the velocity of the air on the upper surface must move at a higher speed. At this higher velocity, the air has less pressure than the slower air passing underneath.

Although the air beneath the wing, which moves more slowly, is at normal pressure, it is higher than the air above the wing and pushes the wing up. If the wing is going through the air fast enough, this helps create lift and allows the bird to leave the ground. The upper surface of a wing is curved. In an animal wing, the upper surface is convex (curved like the outside of a circle), and the lower surface is concave (curved like the inside of a circle).

You can see this most easily in birds and bats, but it is also true in insects. This curvature forms the airfoil needed for flight. The curvature is most pronounced in birds that fly slowly, such as vultures and eagles. In an airplane, both the upper and lower surfaces of the wing are convex. The front edge is rounded, and the back edge is tapered.

The object of creating an airfoil is to have the air pass smoothly over the wing and make flying easier. This applies to both animal wings and airplane wings. When air flows horizontally, its pressure decreases as its speed increases. When the speed is reduced, the pressure increases. The higher pressure under the wing pushes the wing up into the lower pressure area.

Weight and Lift, Thrust and Drag

The study of flight involves four forces: weight, lift, thrust, and drag. In animals, the relationship between these four forces helps determine the design of wings, muscles, and the arrangement of organs.

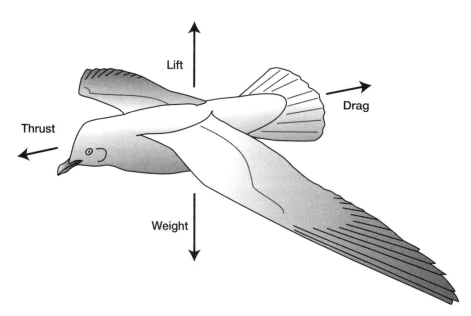

Four forces act on a bird flying at a constant height and speed: weight, lift, thrust, and drag.

Weight is a problem for all animals and machines that fly. Weight always depends on gravity—the force that is pulling them toward Earth. To fly, animals (and people) need to reduce their weight as much as possible.

Usually, weight reduction involves the development of special lightweight body coverings, such as the feathers on bird wings or the scales on butterfly wings. Bats, which have body hair like other mammals, including people, have very little hair on their wings. In birds, changes involve reducing the weight of the skeleton as much as possible without the loss of structural strength (see Chapter 3). In airplanes, engineers have accomplished the same thing by using lightweight aluminum instead of heavier steel.

The wings, which are airfoils, create *lift*. The air speeding over the wing moves faster over the top than the bottom and provides the force needed to get off the ground. Wings are curved, so that there is more surface area across the top than underneath. The air moving across the top of the wing moves faster than the air going underneath the wing, providing lift.

When a bird takes off, it faces into the wind and adjusts the curvature of its wings. This creates an area of low air pressure above the wing and sometimes this provides enough force to lift the bird off the ground. When there is no wind, the bird must create lift by running or jumping. Watch

Lift from Airfoils

The shape of an airfoil helps create lift. You can see this by building a simple model of an airplane wing. A plane's wing is different from a bird or bat wing because the undersurface of an animal's wing is concave. Your model will be flat.

Cut a strip of paper $2\frac{3}{8}$ inches wide by 10 inches long (6 cm by 26 cm). Fold it so that the bottom is $1\frac{3}{4}$ inches (4 cm) longer than the top. Tape the top to the bottom, leaving a single bottom edge. Put a ruler through the fold. Hold the wing up and blow across the top surface, from the folded side to the single-layer side. Watch how the wing reacts to the relative speed of the wind over the upper and lower surfaces.

ducks or geese take off from a pond or pigeons take off from the ground to see these birds creating lift.

The force that propels the animal through the air is called *thrust*. In animals, the muscles and wings generate thrust. In birds and bats, the muscles are in the chest. Birds have a large breastbone that allows for the attachment of flight muscles. In airplanes, the engine produces thrust, and the wings produce lift.

The friction of air against a moving body causes *drag*. To reduce drag, an animal such as a bird or bat folds its legs against its body as it flies, and to reduce friction, a larger airplane retracts its landing gear in flight. The smooth, *streamlined* outline of both birds and airplanes reduces air resistance, making it easier for the air to flow around them.

Not all the air that flows over a bird's wing or an airplane wing moves smoothly, however. Sometimes eddies—small "whirlpools" of air—are created at the trailing edge. Eddies, which occur at the wing tips and extend forward along the upper surface of the wing, produce *turbulence*. Researchers use wind tunnels to study how eddies form and how turbulence develops. The greater the turbulence, the greater the drag.

Scientists sometimes build models using either air or water to help understand the way a fluid flows over a surface—to see how air moves and what it does. Wind tunnels are a way to study animal flight and test aircraft designs. In the process of discovering the principles of airplane design, the Wright brothers constructed the first wind tunnel for aeronautical research. You can recreate their work. (See Projects You Can Do at the back of this book.)

To reduce drag, engineers have streamlined automobiles and trains, as well as airplanes. Look at a picture of a car built 40 years ago and compare it with the shape of a car today. Notice that the lines of the older cars are square and boxy. Modern cars, with their sleek, smooth appearance and rounded lines, are more streamlined. The more fluid shape of today's cars allows them to move more easily through the air at high speed. The most extreme examples are professional drag-racing cars, which are streamlined and low to the ground. If these cars become too aerodynamic, they might even take off at high speeds!

In the 1920s, the smooth sleek look of streamlined designs became associated with progress, and the look became fashionable. Graceful

The fins on the 1961 Ford Fairlane were more for style than improved aerodynamic efficiency.

aerodynamic curves were part of the Art Deco style. Later, many household appliances such as toasters had a curved, streamlined appearance to give them a futuristic look. One screensaver program for computers even pictures a toaster with wings.

And trains have also become far more streamlined, so they can travel at high speeds—100 miles (161 km) per hour or more—more easily. Today, such trains are used throughout Europe and Japan, and they are beginning to appear in the United States.

Angle of Attack

When the air is not moving, animals can create lift by changing the *angle of attack*—the angle of the wing relative to the direction of flight, or the angle at which the wing encounters the wind. Tilting the wings up and exposing more of the lower surface increases this angle. As a result, more air flows across the top of the wing, creating more lift.

All slow-flying animals must overcome *stalling*, a loss of lift that occurs when the smooth flow of air over a wing becomes turbulent, or rough. If a wing is positioned at too steep an angle of attack, lift drops and drag increases sharply. The critical angle for aircraft wings is about 15 degrees—when the angle of attack exceeds this point, stalling occurs. The wing loses lift in the area of turbulence. If lift cannot be recovered, gravity takes over and the aircraft or animal starts to fall. If this continues, it will eventually lose control and crash.

Watch a bird taking off or landing. Notice that the bird changes the angle of its wings as it maneuvers. When it is landing, it is trying to keep the stalling speed as low as possible. Depending on the path the bird takes and on whether it's flying slowly or quickly, certain angles of attack are best.

Wind and Flight Speed

Wind is the result of the uneven heating of the Earth's surface. Pressure and temperature changes that cause horizontal movements of the air as well as upward and downward movements create air currents and wind. Warm air rises, and after the heated air reaches a sufficient altitude to cool, it descends in downdrafts. The cooler, denser air moving horizontally is what we call "wind." The atmosphere tries to maintain equal pressure and temperature between the rising and falling columns of air.

Suppose a person asks how fast a bird or a plane flies. Usually, the answer is given in terms of miles or kilometers per hour. This is the *air speed,* a measure of how fast the object could move without having a wind blow against it and slow it down. This speed is absolute—it doesn't matter what direction the wind is blowing from or how fast it is blowing. Wind direction is relative, depending on the direction of flight. The wind may be blowing in a bird's face—a *head wind*, or coming from behind— a *tail wind*, or from the side—a *beam wind*.

Even if the air is not moving, objects moving through the air "create" their own wind, known as *relative wind.* The wind striking the front of birds and airplanes on calm days is relative wind, just like the wind you feel against your face when you ride a bicycle on a calm day.

The speed of the wind animals encounter has a direct effect on their speed over the ground below—the *ground speed.* Watch a pigeon flying into a strong head wind. The pigeon may be flying at full speed, yet it appears to fly slowly or almost seems to "stand still." The wind is canceling the bird's efforts to travel, reducing its ground speed to almost zero.

Relative speed is the movement of one object in reference to another. When you walk, run, or cycle facing into a strong head wind, your ground speed decreases, but your effort increases. However, if the wind is at your back, you can travel with less effort than if there is no wind at all. The following equations illustrate this relationship:

$$\text{Air speed} - \text{Head wind} = \text{Ground speed}$$

$$\text{Air speed} + \text{Tail wind} = \text{Ground speed}$$

Suppose two birds are flying at the same air speed—20 miles (32 km) per hour—but in opposite directions. The wind is blowing in one bird's face at a speed of 10 miles (16 km) per hour, and the other bird has the same wind at its back. The head wind reduces the ground speed of one bird to 10 miles (16 km) per hour (20 – 10 miles; 32 – 16 km), and the tail wind increases the ground speed of the other to 30 miles (48 km) per hour (20 + 10 miles; 32 + 16 km).

Wind speed and direction are sometimes a factor at outdoor track meets. Officials have ruled that if the wind is blowing at the runners' backs at speeds of more than 4.5 miles per hour (2 meters per second), records cannot be set because the runners' times are "wind-assisted."

Aircraft can take full advantage of a tail wind too, but most birds and other animals prefer some wind from the side, because their entire body is built to provide the most streamlining when they are flying against some wind.

Birds: True Fliers

What Makes Birds Such Good Fliers?

Birds can change altitude and direction at will. Strong flight muscles and highly specialized wings are just two of the many features that allow them to fly so effortlessly. The following description provides information about the structural adaptations that make birds so well suited for flight:

1. True wings—aerodynamic structures that allow flight as the primary means of locomotion in most species. In birds, the wings are the equivalent of arms and hands in people.
2. Feathers—the special lightweight structures on the wings that provide the shape of the airfoil covering. Feathers also cover most of a bird's body and help retain body heat.

The great egret sometimes uses its large, feathered wings as a sunshade while it fishes.

3. A skeleton that is light enough to allow flight yet tough enough to withstand the force of landing. The hollow bones of birds are specially reinforced. In addition, instead of having teeth and heavy jaws, birds have beaks. The size and shape of the beak differs depending on what a particular bird eats. Flamingos have serrated, or notched, beaks with filtering plates that strain algae and small animals out of the water. Eagles have hooked, pointed beaks for tearing meat and fish.

4. Strong muscles in the pectoral area—the shoulder blades, including the wishbone—that are some of the most powerful in nature. The muscles that power the wings are attached to the keel-shaped breastbone and the force is transmitted by the lever and pulley action of bones, tendons, and ligaments. The leg muscles are also located close to the bird's body and the lower leg has a minimum of flesh.

5. Positioning of all heavy muscles at or near the center of gravity. (To find a center of gravity, balance a pencil on your finger. When the pencil balances, the part that rests on your finger is the pencil's center of gravity. If you could hold a bird the same way you hold the pencil, you could determine the bird's center of gravity.) The bird's internal organs, such as

the heart, lungs, stomach, liver, and intestines, are compactly grouped in the center of the body cavity.

6. High body temperature, which allows vigorous muscular activity at all times. Birds, like humans, are warm-blooded, which means that they regulate their body temperature internally. Normally, birds have a higher body temperature than humans do.

7. Air sacs that provide a complete exchange of air with each breath. The air sacs also help regulate the bird's body temperature by allowing the ventilation of excess heat. In some bird species, the respiratory system is synchronized with flight movements. As the bird flaps its wings, it breathes. This action provides all parts of the bird with the oxygen necessary for maximum energy production.

8. Blood that is efficient at carrying oxygen. The high content of red blood cells enables these cells to carry oxygen from the lungs to the muscles.

9. A streamlined body that keeps drag at a minimum.

A "Human" Bird

What do you suppose a birdlike human would look like? We would need to make many major changes, besides the obvious need for wings and feathers.

First, the birdlike person would have a deep, broad chest. The person would have to trade their powerful legs and arms for an equal amount of muscle in the chest. If you look at a chicken's breast you see the largest single group of muscles in the bird's body.

Second, the person would have to reduce the thickness of their legs and completely change their feet. Think of a chicken's legs—they are thin, and the leg muscles in the "drumstick" are small. A chicken also walks on small feet with three large toes in front and one behind. By contrast a human walks like a bear—on relatively flat feet.

Third, a flying person would have to exchange the solid bones of a modern human for thin, strong bones like the aluminum tubes in a bicycle frame. Other internal changes would include structures that help cool the body when flying humans flap their wings. A more efficient cooling system is needed because flapping takes a great deal of energy and generates large amounts of heat. And in order to balance the weight of the body, organs in the digestive, urinary, and reproductive systems would have to be rearranged.

Finally, the size of the head and the size of the teeth would have to be smaller to reduce the weight our wings would have to carry. The head, including the skull and brain, would have to be taller—to make room for the human brain—and flat-sided to reduce drag. A flying human would need different senses than the ones we use now. In almost all birds the sense of smell is reduced and replaced by keener senses of vision and hearing. For flying humans, this would mean that our faces would change—our noses would be smaller and our eyes would be bigger. A beak with few or no teeth would complete the streamlining of the body.

In short, a human who could fly like a bird would have to be shaped very differently than a person is today. There's more to flying than simply strapping on a pair of wings!

Feathers: Unique to Birds

Only birds have feathers. Their feathers distinguish them from all other groups of animals. Birds shed these important structures at least once a year in a process called molting.

Most of the feathers you see on adult birds are *contour feathers*—body feathers with a hook-and-barb system, something like Velcro that keeps the feathers smooth. This system of interlocking hooks makes the feathers more aerodynamic—more streamlined. The front edge of the wing is bent, and each row of feathers overlaps the next to form an airfoil. Birds preen, or groom, themselves by running their beaks through their feathers to reset any barbs that have become displaced. If you look at a bird from its head to its tail, you will see that each feather overlays the next. Birds have a sleek appearance, with no furlike fuzz.

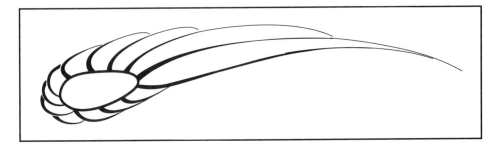

A cross-section of a bird wing shows how the feathers overlap to form an airfoil.

The long contour feathers on a bird's wings and tail are flight feathers. The *shaft* in the middle is off center—the feather is wider on one side than the other. The primary flight feathers are pointed and asymmetrical. The secondary flight feathers lie next to the primaries, a bit closer to the bird's body. The shorter covert feathers overlay the flight feathers on both the upper and lower wing surfaces. Covert feathers help give the wings their aerodynamic shape. Skin muscles twist the flight feathers to the correct angle for each part of the wing beat.

The soft downy feathers are part of the bird's insulation system. Unlike the flight feathers, they have barbs but no hooks. These are the feathers that people use in jackets, comforters, and pillows.

How Feathered Wings Work

When you look at the general shape of a bird, you can see how the parts merge to form a flying animal. The broad chest, the widest part of the

The housefly can dart around, flying forward, backward, and sideways.

The four wings of the northern emerald darterfly, which are almost transparent, provide great control and maneuverability.

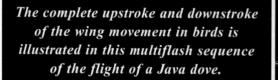

The complete upstroke and downstroke of the wing movement in birds is illustrated in this multiflash sequence of the flight of a Java dove.

The broad wings of the white admiral butterfly allow it to fly slowly and sometimes even glide.

For the albatross, landing is often difficult, and a controlled crash may occur. Because of this awkwardness, the albatross is often called the "gooney bird."

The swallow has sharply pointed wings, like those of a fighter plane, that are suited to maneuvering in tight spaces.

The albatross uses its long slender wings to soar over land and water.

The bald eagle lands with its wings and tail spread.

The bald eagle, which can see about six times better than humans, can locate its prey from high above the ground. People may be called "eagle-eyed" if they can see especially well.

The barn owl has soft feathers on its wings that act as silencers so the owl's wings make no noise when they flap. This way, the owl can hunt stealthily.

Birds may use their feathers for display as well as for flight. Male peacocks spread their tail feathers to impress females during courtship.

body, tapers back toward the tail. The wings form the shape of a fan. When a bird spreads its wings, the primary feathers are those toward the end of the wing, the secondary feathers are in the middle, and the tertiary feathers are closest to the body.

These three types of feathers present a smooth, wide flight surface. The feathered wings provide both lift and thrust. The sections closer to the body provide lift, while those farther away produce thrust. When a bird flies, it positions its wings at the angle that gives the most lift with the least effort. The speed at which the wings flap produces the thrust.

The outer half of the bird's wing—the part that lies away from the body— is the propulsion unit. During flapping flight, it makes a "figure eight." The wing moves forward and downward, pulling the bird along. The next movement, an upward and backward motion, pushes the bird through the air. In all birds, the part of the wing closer to the body moves only slightly and prevents the bird from bobbing up and down in flight. However, some birds normally fly in an up-and-down manner, not because of any damage to their wings.

A bird that is coming in for a landing, or "stopping" to pick something out of the air, may need to extend its *alula,* a specialized set of stiff feathers on the front, or leading, edge of a bird's wing. The alula forms a space between the alula feathers and the front edge of the wing. In normal flight, the alula is tucked out of the way, but when a bird encounters turbulence or approaches stalling speed, it spreads the alula forward to make a space between the feathers and the leading edge of the wing. These spaces help prevent stalling and increase lift—they allow the air to flow faster and more evenly, thus reducing turbulence. Spaces between the outermost primary feathers make flight smoother.

The alula on the wing of a white dove is clearly visible as it comes in for a landing.

41

A bird *hovers* by facing into the wind and reducing its speed until it matches that of the wind. Although it may still be flapping its wings, it is almost motionless in relation to the ground. However, this is different from the flying action of a hummingbird, which can truly hover in midair. The body of the hummingbird is inclined at a steep angle to the horizontal, allowing the wings to move through the air in a near-horizontal plane, like the rotor blades of a helicopter.

In animals and aircraft, wings may be short and wide for slow-speed flight or long and narrow for long-distance flying. The wing span is the distance from wing tip to wing tip. Long narrow wings, like those of the albatross, are perfect for gliding. Long wide wings, like those of a vulture, are just right for soaring. Sharply pointed wings, like those of a swallow, are best for swift flight.

Descendants of Dinosaurs

Where did birds come from? Not from pterosaurs, even though these reptiles could fly. Experts disagree about the origin of birds. One group of scientists claims that birds developed from small, meat-eating dinosaurs, such as *Velociraptor,* and another group believes that birds developed from the reptilian ancestors of dinosaurs. The possible presence of feathers and featherlike structures in dinosaurs makes this a controversial topic. (See the To Find Out More section at the back of this book for more information.)

The fossil *Archaeopteryx,* discovered in 1861, is the closest example of a "missing link" between dinosaurs and birds yet to be found. This prehistoric creature, which lived in the early Jurassic Period (about 140 million years ago), had features of both birds and reptiles. *Archaeopteryx* may have been able to fly a little.

For such a small animal, *Archaeopteryx* had a huge impact on the science world. Charles Darwin's important book about evolution, *The Origin of Species,* was published in 1859, two years before the fossil of *Archaeopteryx* was actually discovered. At that time, few fossils showed any shared characteristics between two different classes of animals. *Archaeopteryx* became one of the first fossils used to demonstrate evolutionary theory.

An examination of the fossil specimen *Archaeopteryx* shows a few modifications from the original reptilian design. The creature can be

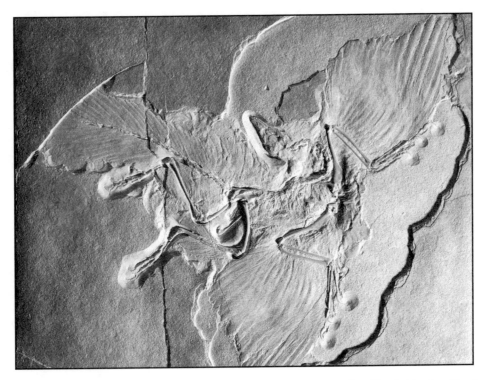

Note the clear impression of feathers on the wings and tail of this fossil of Archaeopteryx, *a primitive bird. A bony tail and teeth are signs of this animals reptilian ancestry.*

thought of as a bird with dinosaur features such as a long, bony tail, or a dinosaur with bird features such as feathers. *Archaeopteryx* was more like dinosaurs than like birds in the following ways:

1. Like dinosaurs, *Archaeopteryx* had teeth in its bill. Modern birds have no teeth.
2   Like dinosaurs, *Archaeopteryx* had solid bones. Modern birds have hollow bones with air cavities and special supports.
3. Like dinosaurs, *Archaeopteryx* had bones in its tail. Modern birds have tails without bones.
4. Like dinosaurs, *Archaeopteryx* did not have a deep, keel-shaped breastbone for the attachment of the flight muscles. Modern birds have such a breastbone.

So what did *Archaeopteryx* have in common with modern birds? It had asymmetrical flight feathers, just like birds today.

During the 1990s, scientists made many new discoveries of fossil birds and birdlike dinosaurs, some of which may predate *Archaeopteryx*. For example, the fossil dinosaur *Sinosauropteryx* was found in China in early Cretaceous deposits estimated to be about 70 million years old. It has thin fibers at the hips and tail, which some researchers think may be feathers or featherlike structures. *Sinosauropteryx* is the oldest dinosaur to have evidence of feathers, although it had no other adaptations for flight.

Scientists later found *Caudipteryx*, another fossil bird, in the same area. It has clear impressions of feathers on the arms and tail but was not built to fly. Another fossil from the same region, *Protarchaeopteryx,* has symmetrical feathers. It may have been able to glide but does not appear to have been capable of flapping flight.

The boundary between modern birds and their dinosaur ancestors is a hazy one. As more fossils help fill in the gaps in the bird-dinosaur family tree, scientists are reassessing their understanding of the origin of birds.

Not All Birds Fly

Usually, birds are the first animals that come to mind when people think of flight in animals. But not all birds can fly. Some birds have adapted to other forms of locomotion. For example, penguins "fly" underwater using the same wing movements that other birds use in the air. Penguins' wings now serve as flippers. Other birds, such as the flightless cormorants that inhabit the Galapagos Islands, lost the ability to fly when they adapted to their isolated home, 600 miles (965 km) from South America. Species may lose the ability to fly during the process of evolution.

For example, the ostrich is a flightless bird that has only wing stubs. It moves by running along the ground at speeds of 30 miles (50 km) per hour. Like other related flightless birds, such as rheas, emus, kiwis, and cassowaries, the ostrich has tiny wings and lacks many other flight specializations, such as a deep breastbone and flight feathers. The moa of New Zealand and the elephant bird of Madagascar—birds in the same group as ostriches—are extinct.

The fossil record includes many species of huge birds, such as a giant condor called *Teratornis incredibilis* that lived in California. With

A Giant Bird

According to an Arabian legend, a giant bird known as the rukh, or roc, once inhabited an island in the Indian Ocean. The explorer Marco Polo reported that Kublai Khan, the Mongol emperor of China, was once given a rukh feather. A tale in *The Arabian Nights* describes how the sailor Sinbad encountered the bird:

> *I beheld a white dome, of prodigious height and extent...I found it to be very smooth...it was at least fifty paces around. All of a sudden the sky became dark as if it had been covered with a thick cloud...I found it occasioned by a bird of monstrous size...I had often heard mariners speak of a miraculous bird called the roc...the great dome must be its egg...*[1]

Several species of giant birds—called "elephant birds"—that lived in Madagascar were the basis of this fabulous story. *Aepyornis titan*, the largest member of this group, was 10 feet (3 m) tall and weighed about 1,000 pounds (450 kg). Its eggs were the largest ever laid by any animal—35 inches (89 cm) in circumference.

a wingspan of 16 to 17 feet (4.9 to 5.2 m), it may have been the largest flying bird ever known. During the Ice Age more than 12,000 years ago, animals sometimes became mired in the tar pits in what is present-day Los Angeles. The vultures who came to feed on them also became trapped if their feathers got stuck. Many of the specimens of *T. incredibilis* found in the tar pits are on display at a Los Angeles museum. Even today, animals get stuck in the tar pits in front of the museum.

Hovering Hummingbirds

Have you ever seen a hummingbird darting among flowers or zooming into a feeder? These remarkable birds may be small, but they are always busy. Known for their brilliant plumage, hummingbirds can hover over a flower to drink nectar for as long as they want. They can also fly in all directions—

forward, backward, and sideways. To fly horizontally, hummingbirds tilt their wings to force the air backward and create thrust as well as lift. To fly backward, hummingbirds rotate their wings behind their backs to push the air in front of them. To fly in any other direction, hummingbirds adjust the angle of their wings to move air in the opposite direction.

Several features make the specialized flight of hummingbirds possible.

1. About 30 percent of a hummingbird's weight is flight muscle—a higher percentage (based on weight) than any other bird. Because hummingbirds obtain full power from both the upward and downward strokes of their wings, the two sets of muscles are almost equal in size.

2. The hummingbird's propellerlike wing is attached to the shoulder and it can swivel, permitting the hummingbird to generate lift on the upstroke as well as on the downstroke.

3. The hummingbird beats its wings more than 70 times per second—a higher rate than any other bird. Hummingbirds use an incredible amount of energy. If they don't eat daily, they may die.

Hummingbird Observation

The easiest way to attract hummingbirds is to set up a feeder. Place the feeder near a window and use good commercial hummingbird food. Keep the feeder clean and filled, because the birds become dependent on the food source. Once hummingbirds find the feeder, they will visit it regularly.

Record the behavior of the hummingbirds. Use a bird book to identify them, and record the dates and times you see them. Notice whether the birds share the feeder or fight over it.

To provide a more permanent food source, you can plant a hummingbird garden. Then you can watch hummingbirds at work without having to clean and refill a feeder. An assortment of flowers and a source of drinking water will attract hummingbirds, bees, and butterflies—you'll have a variety of animal aviators to observe. (See the To Find Out More section at the back of this book for more information.)

Other Animal Aviators: Insects and Bats

Three groups of animals—birds, insects, and bats—have developed the ability to use true flapping flight. Insects were the first such animals to become true fliers. The flight mechanisms used by insects are totally different from those used by birds and bats, which are vertebrates—animals with backbones. People have studied birds for centuries and understand how they fly, but intensive investigation of insect flight is just beginning.

One of the most puzzling aspects of insect flight is that their wings seem too small to create the necessary lift. An old saying tells of an engineer who said that bumblebees cannot fly. But this never stopped these insects from taking off!

Insects: The First Fliers

Insects can fly in all directions and in all sorts of ways for all sorts of reasons. Dragonflies catch prey on the wing. Honeybees fly to collect food from flowers and to begin new colonies. Ants and termites may not fly until they are reproductive adults and need to mate. House flies zip around to feed on organic material, and they can even land upside down!

Our present understanding of flight does not apply to insects. Unlike birds and bats, which have wings that are modified arms and hands, insects' wings contain neither muscles nor tendons. These seemingly flat structures do not appear to be typical airfoils.

But when insect wings begin to flap, and the air begins to move around them, they become curved and more aerodynamic. When necessary, they flex along fold lines, like pleats in a fan. The pleat lines radiate from the base of the wing near the thorax—the middle segment of the insect's body. This allows the insect to carry a large membranous wing in a minimum of space. (See the Projects You Can Do section at the back of this book for information about a project involving pleats and insect wings.) The wings are hinged so that they can move freely in almost any direction.

Insects have a hard exoskeleton on the outside of their bodies, and their legs and wings are attached to the thorax. Like the exoskeleton, the wings are composed of chitin—a flexible, strong substance similar to the material in your fingernails. The veins of the wings provide structural support, carry nerve impulses, and keep the wings supplied with blood.

Unlike aircraft, which may stall at angles of attack of about 15 degrees, insects can achieve much greater angles of attack—up to 60 degrees—before they begin to stall. Insects seem able to delay a stall using a four-part wing movement. Not only do the wings move up and down, but they also rotate in a flipping motion. At high angles of attack, the front, or leading, edge of the wing generates a vortex—a small whirlpool of air. Air flow along the axis of the wing stabilizes the vortex, and this action contributes to lift during the downstroke. In some ways, this "wing flipping" resembles the movements of bats in flight.

The wings of insects, such as the honeybee, are much thinner and flatter than those of birds. Honeybees can hover over flowers while they collect nectar, which they use to make honey. They may also gather pollen, which they transfer to another flower on other nectar-gathering visits.

One scientist has described insect flight this way. "Most insects flap their wings forward and backward, not up and down. The wings move through the air like flattened hands sweeping to and fro. The thumb-side edge would be tilted upward into the oncoming flow, and between strokes, the wings flip, as if the hands were to change from palm down to palm up or vice versa."[1]

With their large wings, dragonflies fly between 19 and 38 miles (30 and 60 km) per hour. Honeybees fly at speeds of 25 miles (40 km) per hour, and house flies travel through the air at the relatively slow speed of 4.5 miles (7.2 km) per hour.

During "speed flight," the fastest flight of monarch butterflies, the insects may travel at speeds as high as 22 to 30 miles (36 to 48 km) per hour.

With a tail wind of 20 miles (32 km) per hour, they can reach speeds of almost 50 miles (80 km) per hour! The bending of their broad wings helps them increase their forward speed.

Scientists have categorized other types of monarch flight. Gliding flight, which is similar to the gliding of other large-winged animals, is a slow form of flight that requires less effort. On calm days, you may see monarch butterflies gliding. Cruising flight is another pattern of slow flight that involves gliding. The butterflies use it when they are foraging (looking for food) and during long-distance flight.

Bats: Mammals on the Wing

Bats are the only mammals that can actually fly. Because bats often spend time hanging upside down, they just need to let go to take off. A bat's front feet, or "hands," have evolved into wings, and skin stretches between the elongated fingers. Also, membranous skin flaps that extend between the body, including the tail, and the legs form one large wing. A network of elastic fibers further strengthens the wings.

The elongated finger bones of the long-eared bat act as supports for the wings.

Both bats and birds have developed some of the same specializations for flight.

1. Both bats and birds have wings that are modified arms and hands.
2. Both bats and birds have lightweight skeletons with large areas for the attachment of flight muscles.
3. Birds have specialized feathers covering their wings to help them fly. Bats have skin covering their wings, but most have little hair.
4. Both birds and bats have muscles that allow them to control the shape of their wings in flight. In birds, almost all wings muscles attach to the keel-shaped breastbone. In bats, several muscles in the chest power the wings, but only one muscle is attached to the breastbone.
5. Both groups have elliptical bodies that are streamlined to move efficiently through the air.
6. Both groups have highly efficient cooling systems that allow them to lose the excess heat they generate from rapid flying.

In bats, as in small birds, the downstroke is the power stroke, and the upstroke is a recovery movement. During the downstroke, the bat spreads its wings fully and holds them at a steady angle of attack. The area of the wing away from the body provides thrust, especially the membrane between the third and fourth fingers. As speed increases, the air pressure is greater at the wing tip. The flexible wing responds to the increased pressure by lagging behind, and the air pressure twists the wing tip. The air is then forced backward, resulting in thrust.

During the upstroke, the wing is flexed with the wing coming upward and a little backward. The airstream moving past the animal aids movement. The part of the wing closer to the body acts as a lifting surface. This part of the wing may also help hold the bat level in flight, just as it does in birds.

You can imitate the way bats fly by moving your arms in a certain way. Hold them out, parallel to the ground. Pull your arms upward to begin the upstroke, bending them slightly at the elbow. The primary thrust is coming from the area closest to your body. When your hands reach halfway to your head, reverse the movement. Straighten your arms completely to begin the downstroke, pulling down and back. Now the primary thrust is coming from the part of your arms furthest from your body. Stop when your arms are parallel to the ground, and repeat the upstroke. If you could move your arms quickly enough, your hands would tend to trail behind them.

Humans can't quite duplicate the movement of the wings of bats, because these flying creatures can change the curvature of their wings. Also, the wings of bats have more surface area than you have in your arms, and they generate more thrust than you could.

Like birds, each group of bats has a wing design suited to the type of flying it does. Some of the flying foxes, the large, slow-flying, fruit-eating bats of Australia, Africa, and Asia, have a wing span of 5 feet (1.5 m). Most bats also have broad, short wings, which means that they can fly slowly, with precise control. Bats that fly fast and stay in the air longer have narrower, longer wings. Mexican free-tail bats can fly at speeds of 60 miles (97 km) per hour. The insectivorous, or insect-eating, bats of the genus *Rhinolophus* are swift fliers and important members of the ecosystem. They help control the mosquito population—one bat can eat hundreds of the annoying insects! The fish-eating bats of tropical Central and South America are powerful fliers that can "gaff" fish—pluck them right out of the water.

Like some birds, such as hummingbirds, some bats can hover, which is especially useful when feeding on flower nectar. Bats pollinate some plants—big, white flowers that are open at night may be bat-pollinated. When bats hover, the upstroke is directed forward, and the downstroke is directed backward. The wing movement is reversed from level flight. In the upstroke the wing tip is turned over, so that the upper surface is turned down. The leading edge of the wing still leads. At the end of the upstroke, the reversed tip is rapidly flipped backward, producing upward thrust. The downstroke is similar to that of a hummingbird in level flight.

Bats can control the shape of their wings to an even greater extent than birds can. They use the muscles and bones in the wings to adjust the shape of the airfoil, including its curvature. This provides high lift at slow speeds and tremendous maneuverability. The double-layered skin membrane on the leading edge of the wing can be sloped downward to form flaps, which per- form the same function as those on a plane. They improve the efficiency of the wing by increasing lift. They also help bats avoid stalling, just as the alula does in birds. Leading-edge flaps are particularly effective in bats with thin wings that have thin leading edges.

Batty Ideas

Bats are difficult to study because they are usually active at night. However, bats need places to rest or sleep, and you can build a bat house by using the plans available from Bat Conservation International (BCI) (see the To Find Out More section at the back of this book). Note which bats stay in your bat house. Observe the bats when they go out to feed at sunset. To discover what species of insects they might be eating, set up a white sheet and project a light on it. Insects are attracted to the light, and you can identify them with the help of a good insect guide.

Mounting a bat house on a building or tall pole encourages bats to take up residence.

53

Chapter 5

Migration:
Long-Distance Flight

Many animals have a remarkable ability to return to the same place every year at a specific time. This seasonal cycle is known as *migration*. Birds, bats, and insects, which all have the ability to fly, make extensive migrations. Why do animals migrate? Perhaps a place has become uninhabitable—too cold, for example—and the animals want to move to a warmer location. Sometimes they travel to their breeding grounds to mate and reproduce.

Experts know that migrating animals use several navigational aids—the sun, stars, and surface features of the Earth, such as rivers. However, exactly how they navigate over unknown territory and reach their goal is still a mystery. Continuing scientific research will tell us more about how animals perceive the world and how they navigate.

Bird Migration

Bird migration is a fascinating subject, and how birds find their way back to their nesting sites every year is not yet known. Some birds, such as many cardinals, sparrows, and blue jays, remain in the same habitat year-round. Birds that migrate in a north-south direction in response to changes in temperature and day length are probably the most familiar, such as those birds that spend the winter in the southern United States but return to Canada to breed.

What Is High?

Most species of insects and bats fly within a limited range of altitude. Even migratory species of insects, such as the monarch butterfly, do not normally cross high mountain ranges. "High altitude" is a relative term. To a person living in Colorado, a state with a high average elevation, "high altitude" may refer to parts of the Rocky Mountains over 10,000 feet (3,049 m) high. But to a person living at sea level, even the lowest point in Colorado (3,350 feet [1,021 m]) may seem high. In this book, any altitude greater than 1 mile (1.6 km), or 5,280 feet (1,610 m), is considered high.

The lower the elevation, the more air is pressing down on you, held in place by the Earth's gravity. At high altitudes, the air is lighter and less dense. At sea level, the average atmospheric pressure is 14.7 pounds per square inch (29.9 inches of mercury on a barometer). As the elevation increases, the atmospheric pressure decreases—along with the temperature. Even in tropical areas, if you climb high enough, you eventually find freezing temperatures and snow. For example, there is snow on Mount Kilimanjaro, the highest mountain in Africa at 19,340 feet (5,895 m) all year long—it is located almost right on the equator.

However, some mountain climbers in the Himalayas have seen geese migrating over the peaks. These birds have specialized respiratory and circulatory systems that allow them to adapt to the thin, rarefied atmosphere, which contains less oxygen than it does at sea level. The thin atmosphere provides less lift, and birds must use more energy to fly. Because there is less air to push against, birds must flap their wings faster to keep themselves airborne.

The high-flying geese are not the only birds that fly at high altitudes. Using radar, scientists have found that shorebirds migrate from the Maritime

Like other geese, snow geese fly in a "V" formation. The bird at the point of the "V" works hardest, and when it begins to tire, another one takes its place.

Provinces of Canada to the Caribbean at an altitude of more than 1 mile (1.6 km) over Nova Scotia. As many as 10 percent of the migrating birds reportedly travel at altitudes of $2^1/_2$ to 4 miles (4 to 6.4 km) above sea level. Researchers have tracked small perching birds crossing Puerto Rico at altitudes of $2^1/_2$ to more than 3 miles (4 to 5 km).

Unlike humans, birds can fly at high altitudes without having to take the time to adapt to them. Remarkably, birds that live at sea level can fly immediately to high altitudes and then fly hundreds of miles without resting. But weather may be a problem. Strong winds can blow them off course, or tall structures, such as radio towers or buildings, may be obstacles.

Records of bird migration, including studies of homing pigeons, go back nearly 1,000 years, and research continues today. To determine migration routes, researchers put numbered metal bands on birds' legs. (The bands do not interfere with the birds' movements.) The color of the bands is visible at a distance. The actual banding requires special training, and only certain people can do it. However, you may be able to provide assistance (and you can find out whether you want to band birds someday).

Reports of banded birds or the recovery of dead banded birds help researchers learn about migratory patterns. Using the information on the markers, the person who catches the bird contacts the person or organization whose name appears on the band, giving the date the bird was found and the bird's location.

Two birds—the Eskimo curlew and the homing pigeon—have taught us much about bird migration. The Eskimo curlew, a rare bird, migrates from northern Canada to southern Chile and Argentina and back. To obtain insight into the senses birds use to fly in certain directions, though, work with homing pigeons is more useful.

The Eskimo Curlew

Today, the Eskimo curlew is rare, and scientists and bird-watchers alike sit up and take notice if they hear of a reported sighting. The birds breed at high latitudes in northern Canada—in Nunivak (formerly the Northwest Territories). From 1862 to 1865, a man named Roderick Ross MacFarlane discovered nesting sites in the Bathurst Peninsula and along Franklin Bay. The birds, eggs, and other specimens he collected became the property of the Smithsonian Institution in Washington, D.C.

From its nesting grounds, Eskimo curlews migrate to the Maritime Provinces of Canada. Today, the very small number of Eskimo curlews that survive are probably still preparing for their remarkable journey by feeding on plants, such as the crowberry bush. When the winds and weather are right, Eskimo curlews fly across the western Atlantic Ocean to the Caribbean coast of South America. In the 1800s, the birds reportedly flew to the pampas, or grasslands, near Buenos Aires, Argentina, although the exact site is not known. Once they are in South America, the birds continue to fly south into Patagonia, a region in southern Argentina and southern Chile.

In the spring, Eskimo curlews leave Patagonia and fly to Mexico by an unknown route, arriving on the Yucatan Peninsula and then flying to Texas. From there, they follow the western drainage of the Mississippi River and return to their Arctic breeding grounds.

Before Eskimo curlews were hunted to the point of extinction, they could be seen in large numbers. In the late 1800s, people shot the birds on the Atlantic coast of Canada and the United States during the fall migration,

The Arctic tern, which migrates thousands of miles each year, spends the summer in the Arctic and the winter in the Antarctic.

and along the Mississippi drainage during the spring migration. In Kansas, the slaughter was so great that people heaped the dead birds into piles like mounds of coal.

As a result, the Eskimo curlew is an endangered species today, which means that it is in immediate danger of becoming extinct if it is not protected. Now the Eskimo curlew is completely protected along its migration route, but people rarely see the bird. Bird-watchers keep a close eye out in Texas, especially on the coast at Galveston Island. Since 1945, people have occasionally spotted Eskimo curlews at Galveston.

Eskimo curlews are not the only birds that fly long distances. Many other species fly thousands of miles each year. The Arctic tern, the bird with the longest known migration route, makes an annual round trip of up to 22,000 miles (35,400 km). It flies between the Arctic, where it spends the summer, and the Antarctic, where it spends the winter (summer in the Southern Hemisphere). Except while Arctic terns are breeding, in the coastal areas in of northern North America, they spend most of their lives on the wing.

The Homing Pigeon

Unlike the Eskimo curlew, the homing pigeon—a domesticated form of the wild European rock dove—is a common, easily observed bird. Until the invention of the telegraph and, later, radio, homing pigeons were one of the fastest ways to send a message over long distances. Pigeons have a remarkable "homing instinct." No matter where these birds are released, they always fly straight home to their mates and their young— homing pigeons mate for life. Both male and female homing pigeons play a role in raising the young and either males or females can be used to carry messages.

During World War I (1914–1918), American and Allied armed forces released pigeons with cameras strapped to their bodies to take aerial photographs. Until the end of World War II (1939–1945), many armies used homing pigeons to carry messages. The most recent use of homing pigeons occurred during the Gulf War in 1991, when the United States and its allies fought Iraq's forces in Kuwait. Pigeon coops were found in Iraqi trenches.

Researchers have discovered that homing pigeons use several navigational systems when they fly. During the day, they use the sun as a reference, just as other birds do. As the day progresses, they are able to correct for the change in the sun's position. At night, they use the stars.

When the sky is overcast, pigeons use polarized light as a directional aid and a supplement to navigational information obtained at other times. Polarized light vibrates in only one direction, unlike natural light. Pigeons have a polarizing filter in their eyes.

Homing pigeons can also use the Earth's magnetic field to find their way. Each bird has a small amount of magnetite, a type of magnetic iron ore, at the base of its skull, so that it is sensitive to the Earth's magnetic field.

Because pigeons were so important at one time, pigeon breeding has become an art. Today, people continue to maintain pigeon breeds called "racing homers" for racing purposes. Some pigeons races are over 500 or 600 miles (800 or 960 km) long. The pigeons you can see in urban areas are not the same as the pure-bred racing pigeons that breeders have worked so hard to raise. Although these common pigeons can certainly navigate from place to place, they cannot fly as far as racing pigeons. Nevertheless, they are wonderful animals, and by watching them, you can learn a lot about bird flight.

Pigeon Projects

Even if you don't breed pigeons, you can do all kinds of projects with them. The Cornell University Laboratory of Ornithology operates a program called Pigeon Watch, which has organized projects that require only observation. (See the To Find Out More section at the back of this book.)

If you want to become more involved with pigeons, you may wish to join a pigeon club. Raising homing pigeons is not an expensive hobby, and it allows you to learn more about how the birds fly and navigate. A wide variety of pigeon breeds are easy to work with. Some breeds do acrobatics when they fly, while others are famous for their striking colors. If you are not sure which breed you want, select a few from a book on pigeons and then contact the club that promotes these breeds. Start your own pigeon loft with the help of your local pigeon club.

Bat Migration

Because most bats fly at night, it has been difficult to study them, but researchers use tags and small radio transmitters. Bats find their way in the dark by *echolocation*—emitting high-pitched sound waves and listening for the echoes. The time it takes for the sound to return to the ears of the bat allows the animal to detect obstacles and locate food. People studied the way bats were able to navigate in the dark and developed sonar using the same principles. Besides echolocation, bats may use the stars to travel from place to place. They may also use the Earth's magnetic field.

To avoid winter cold, bats may migrate long distances. For example, Mexican free-tail bats, which are native to central Texas, are one of the few North American bats that do not hibernate. Instead, they migrate to Mexico at the first sign of cold weather, and then return to the southern United States to bear their young. Different groups of bats follow different migration routes, covering distances of up to 620 miles (1,000 km).

At dusk, Mexican free-tail bats emerge from Bracken Cave, Texas, and begin a night of feeding on insects.

When the female bats go to "nursery" caves, the sexes separate, and the male bats *roost* elsewhere. Scientists believe that this may help spread out the population, ensuring that all the bats have enough food. When the young bats are ready to fly, they migrate to Mexico with their mothers.

Near San Antonio, Texas, the Mexican free-tail bat is quickly becoming a tourist attraction. At sunset, visitors may come to Bracken Cave, the summer home of 20 million Mexican free-tail bats, to watch the bats take off for a night's hunting. The roost is protected by law, and visitors must not disturb the bats when they are resting. The organization Bat Conservation International (BCI) is working to locate roosting sites of other bat species so that they also can receive protection. (See the To Find Out More section at the back of this book.)

Insect Migration

In general, insects are not known for periodic migrations. Most insects, which complete more than one reproductive cycle in a season, spend the winter as hibernating adults. Ladybugs and mosquitoes are two examples. They are not capable of the extensive flight necessary for migration.

Some locusts, a type of grasshopper, are well known for their long-distance movements, which involve journeys of 1,400 to 2,000 miles (2,200 to 3,200 km). In general, locusts move from dry areas to places with somewhat greater rainfall. In Africa, the Middle East, and India, as well as in North and South America, locusts migrate in huge swarms, destroying vegetation in the course of their flight.

Honeybees fly long distances only when they swarm, looking for a new home. Scientists don't know how far a single swarm of bees travels—this depends on weather conditions and how quickly the bees can find a suitable place to live. When worker bees are foraging, they may fly up to 8 miles (13 km). At other times, the bees remain close to the hive, leaving only in search of nectar and pollen. Like homing pigeons, honeybees can correct for the change in the sun's position, and they use magnetite and polarized light to navigate.

The monarch butterfly of North America is the only butterfly known to migrate annually—to make such a long, two-way journey. The flight pattern most often used during migration is what scientists call "social flight," which occurs when monarchs seek one another out and follow each other (for reasons other than breeding).

Some monarch butterflies from southern Canada and the United States travel south to Angangueo, Mexico to spend the winter—a round-trip of up to 3,000 miles (4,800 km). Other monarchs spend the winter on the Monterey Peninsula in northern California, where they roost in trees in large groups. In California, the roosting sites in Pacific Grove on the Monterey Peninsula are protected by law. The event has become so important that an annual festival held to welcome the butterflies draws thousands of visitors.

Unlike birds, individual butterflies make the round-trip only once. The monarchs that return to Mexico or California every fall are the great-great-grandchildren of the butterflies that left the previous spring. On the way

Monarch butterflies cluster together in eucalyptus groves in California during migration. Many of these sites are now protected.

north, the butterflies lay eggs, and the young from this next generation follow the same route as their parents. The adults do not teach their offspring the travel route—several weeks separate the generations.

Researchers have devised a lightweight tagging program, which has provided information about the flight paths of migrating monarchs. Tags made of alar (a kind of plastic) are placed on the leading edge of the butterfly's wing. The tag weighs 0.01 grams—only 1/40th the weight of an adult butterfly. (A paper clip weighs about 1 gram, so a monarch butterfly weighs less than one paper clip.)

Because the tag is so light, it has no effect on the flight of the butterfly. Scientists know that an individual butterfly can fly more than 1,240 miles (2,000 km), but no one knows how the butterflies navigate and find the same areas their parents left.

The Monarch Watch program at the University of Kansas is following the migration of monarch butterflies as part of a cooperative program between universities in the United States and Canada. You can obtain the latest information about butterflies in general, and monarchs in particular, from Monarch Watch (see the To Find Out More section at the back of this book).

Chapter 6

Humans Take to the Skies

Legends that involve human flight are found in many parts of the world. According to a Persian legend, King Kai Kawus (who is said to have ruled around 1500 B.C.) flew on a golden throne carried by four eagles. Alexander the Great, the Macedonian king who conquered Persia (now Iran) in 333 B.C., reportedly traveled in a cage pulled by griffins—creatures that were half-lion and half-eagle.

The Chinese invented gunpowder and used it to power rockets in about 1100 A.D.—sometimes for celebration and sometimes for war. Legend has it that an official named Wan-Hoo attempted to fly using 47 large rockets attached to a wicker chair.

Kites are one of most ancient forms of human-engineered flight, dating back to 1000 B.C. in China. However, people did not completely understand

65

Go Fly a Kite

The next time you want to fly through the air, try flying a kite, which is really an airfoil with more surface area on the top than on the bottom. Like a bat's wing, a kite is reinforced from top to bottom (see Chapter 4).

It takes a bit of practice to fly a kite successfully. To launch the kite, hold it into the breeze, or if the wind isn't strong enough, run with it. Once the wind moving over the upper surface is fast enough to reduce the air pressure, lift overcomes gravity, and the kite begins to climb. When there is a breeze, a kite can climb as high as you want it to.

But don't let the kite climb too fast. If the kite becomes too vertical, it will lose lift and begin to fall because the speed of the wind passing over the top of the kite isn't high enough. Pulling on the control string makes the angle smaller. The angle that the kite makes with the air moving toward it and its tail both affect the kite's stability in the air.

how they worked until the nineteenth century. In 1894, the Australian aviation pioneer Lawrence Hargrave invented the box kite by linking four kites together. With his flight of 16 feet (5 m), he demonstrated that it was possibly to build a safe, stable flying machine. It turns out that Wilbur and Orville Wright, the first aviators to develop and fly a fixed-winged aircraft successfully, also flew kites and learned that they could lift humans off the ground.

Flapping Flight

For many years, people tried to fly by copying birds' or bats' wings. They jumped off towers, failed to fly, and sometimes died. It took a long time for people to understand that they didn't have to look like a bird in order to fly like one

One of the first people who seriously considered the possibilities of human-engineered flight was Leonardo da Vinci, the great Italian artist and inventor. Like many people before him, Leonardo looked at birds and wanted to join them. In the late 1400s and early 1500s, he devoted his attention to animal flight. Unlike most others, he began careful studies

Leonardo da Vinci was one of the first people to give human flight serious consideration. Most of his suggestions for human-powered flying machines involved flapping flight.

from which he developed theories, and then conducted experiments to test his ideas. In the course of his studies, he researched and wrote about the importance of the such factors as gravity, pressure, streamlining, and airflow over surfaces. In addition, he compared air and water as two types of fluids.

For Leonardo, the idea of flapping flight was important, and much of his flight-related work involved sketching and building models of an aircraft he called an "ornithopter." Using a bats wing as a basis for this human-powered device, Leonardo added a long tail-like structure for better control. To overcome the inadequate muscle power of humans, he used levers and pulleys that allowed the pilot to flap the wings of the ornithopter and increase the altitude. No reports of any tests of the ornithopter exist today.

Lighter-Than-Air Flight
Balloons

Human-powered flight proved difficult, so people tried to become airborne by using materials that were lighter than the air itself. This technology involved the use of a basket suspended under a bag full of hot air or gas.

The British chemist Henry Cavendish was one of the pioneers of this method. In 1766, he isolated hydrogen gas, which is which is $14\frac{1}{2}$ times lighter than air. The scientist Joseph Black realized that if the gas were enclosed in a membranelike bladder, or sac, it could be used to lift a small basket, but he never tested his theory. The Italian investigator Tiberius Cavallo tried using various animal bladders, and even paper bags, which were too heavy. How could air be used to support a small basket?

On June 4, 1783, brothers Joseph and Étienne Montgolfier of France successfully launched an unoccupied hot-air balloon. Made of paper-lined linen, it was about 35 feet (11 m) in diameter. The balloon rose to a height of 6,562 feet (2,000 m). On September 19, 1783, the brothers repeated their demonstration before King Louis XVI and Queen Marie Antoinette of France. This time the balloon carried a sheep, a rooster, and a duck, who became the first air passengers. The first people to travel in a hot-air balloon were Pilâtre de Rozier, who was also the first person to die in an air accident, and the Marquis d'Arlandes.

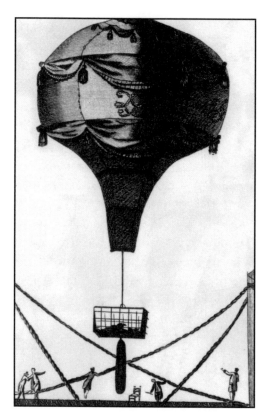

The Montgolfier brothers of France were the first to send a balloon aloft successfully. In a 1783 demonstration, three animals became the first balloon passengers.

68

In their demonstration, the Montgolfier brothers showed that hot air is lighter than cold air. (However, hot air is not as light as hydrogen.) As air heats and expands, it becomes less dense, which makes it lighter than the atmosphere. In a hot-air balloon, a fire is used to heat the air. The pilot in the basket hanging underneath the balloon must regulate the temperature of the air inside the balloon to control how much altitude the balloon gains. If the air inside the balloon cools too much, the balloon will sink. The pilot uses the furnace and ballast, weight that is carried on the balloon, to control its flight. Ballast in the form of bags of sand can be dropped to lighten the load when the balloon needs to rise and the pilot does not want to use the furnace.

After the success of the Montgolfiers, people experimented with improved balloon designs. Some searched for better and safer ways to keep the fires burning, while others looked for new ways of lifting balloons off the ground. Some scientists tried to use the lighter-than-air hydrogen inside a balloon, but no one could develop a material that could contain the hydrogen for sufficiently long periods.

The Montgolfiers hired the French scientist J. A. C. Charles to work on this problem, and on December 1, 1783, Charles successfully launched a balloon that used hydrogen instead of hot air. The balloon was made of rubberized silk. Benjamin Franklin, one of the observers of this first successful hydrogen balloon, wrote to his fellow scientists in the newly independent United States and told them that balloons could be used as high-altitude observation posts. During the American Civil War (1861–1865), President Abraham Lincoln established the first Balloon Corps in the United States Army. The Balloon Corps, which provided some vital information about Confederate troop movements, was disbanded in 1863.

Hot-air and hydrogen balloons can fly, but they have one serious drawback. All balloons are at the mercy of the wind—it is impossible to steer them. In a hot-air balloon, to gain altitude, a pilot can increase the heat of the fire or dump ballast, and to descend, a pilot must allow the air to cool.

Because a hydrogen balloon depends on the lightness of the gas to remain airborne, the only way the pilot can lighten the load and gain altitude is to dump ballast. The only way to land is to let gas escape. The flammability of hydrogen is another problem—it catches fire easily and burns quickly.

Dirigibles

In 1852, a French engineer named Henri Giffard built and tested a cigar-shaped hydrogen balloon powered by a steam engine. The 123-foot (37.5 m)-long balloon traveled at 5 miles (8 km) per hour. Later, investigators used experimental electric motors to power steerable balloons called *dirigibles*. In 1900, the Count Ferdinand von Zeppelin of Germany demonstrated the first dirigible with a rigid, internal structure—a balloon with a skeleton. With the development of gasoline engines, such rigid airships became practical.

In the first part of the twentieth century, dirigibles continued to use hydrogen. During World War I (1914–1918), Germany used airships to bomb London and Paris. However, after World War I, airships were used for peaceful purposes. The firm of Luftschiffbau Zeppelin of Germany became the leading manufacturer of rigid airships and initiated regular passenger service throughout Europe. Britain and the United States also began to construct airships, but after several spectacular crashes, which were usually caused by bad weather, both countries stopped building these aircraft.

The R101, a British-built rigid airship, crashed in 1930.

What Happened to the *Graf Zeppelin?*

It appears that Adolph Hitler of Nazi Germany hated the people who were in charge of the Zeppelin firm, and he was waiting for an opportunity to damage their business. When the *Hindenburg* crashed, Hitler ordered the *Graf Zeppelin* to cancel all its scheduled flights. On the *Graf Zeppelin's* return, Hitler ordered that it be destroyed. Because the Zeppelin company had only two airships, this effectively halted their commercial operations in aviation.

Some zeppelins were a commercial success. The *Graf Zeppelin,* which provided regular passenger service between Europe and South America, never had an accident in all the years it flew—from 1928 to 1937. The *Graf Zeppelin* even made a successful round-the-world flight—nonstop! During its "lifetime," it flew more than 1 million miles (1.6 million km).

Not all zeppelins had the same safety record, however. The *Hindenburg* flew only ten times before it crashed and exploded in flames on May 6, 1937, while landing in Lakehurst, New Jersey. Thirty-five of the 97 people on board, plus 1 member of the ground-crew, lost their lives. A newsreel crew filmed the crash and broadcast the event live on radio. People around the world have seen the film of the disaster. This publicity linked the image of the passenger airship with the crash in the public's mind. Commercial passenger airship service did not resume until the late 1980s, when blimps began taking sightseers on flights around San Francisco Bay.

During the time when the United States was working on airships, scientists realized that the gas helium is lighter than air, but not as light as hydrogen. But helium has one big advantage over hydrogen—helium does not burn. During the late 1930s, the Zeppelin firm asked the United States to sell it some helium, so that it could use the less dangerous gas in its commercial airships. The United States refused, because many people remembered the zeppelin raids of World War I. They were afraid the German government would use the airships as weapons.

Nonrigid airships called *blimps* took over from the giant rigid airships. Blimps, which do not have an internal metal skeleton, are basically bags of gas that use helium gas for lift. Like balloons, blimps can be deflated and rolled up for storage. Blimps are less efficient than the hydrogen-based airships, but they are less of a fire hazard too. Today, blimps are used for advertising and television broadcasting.

The rigid airship, which now uses helium, is making a comeback. In 1998, the Zeppelin firm tested a new cargo-carrying rigid airship that can carry 160 tons. To mark the 100th anniversary of Count Zeppelin's flight, commercial airship service—cargo only, for the time being—has begun in Germany. The dirigible rejoins the blimp, another lighter-than-air aircraft, as a means of air travel.

Heavier-Than-Air Flight

Unpowered Flight: Gliding

While some people were using forms of air travel that involved lighter-than-air flight, other researchers were building flying machines that used the principles of heavier-than-air flight. Lighter-than-air flight has many disadvantages. Balloons are completely at the mercy of the winds, and airships are hard to control in storms. Neither type of aircraft exhibits the mastery of flight associated with birds.

Sir George Cayley, an English scientist, became interested in flight in 1783, at the age of 10, when he learned of the successful balloon tests by the Montgolfier brothers. As a young man, he began experimenting with and building gliders. He later developed a machine to test the flow of air over various types of wings. During his career, Cayley conducted much of the research and wrote many of the scientific papers that became the basis of modern flight theory. (For an explanation of the principles that form the basis of modern aerodynamics, see Chapter 2.) Experts have stated that "Cayley identified the forces of lift, drag, and thrust as they applied to aviation; developed the cambered (curved) upper surface on a wing to increase lift; and worked on propellers and power plants."[1]

In addition, Cayley conceived of biplanes and triplanes and the different roles they might play. Biplanes have two-part wings, one above the other. Wilbur and Orville Wright's plane, the *Flyer*, was a biplane. In World War I, biplanes were standard. The crop dusters you see today are biplanes—these agile aircraft can fly at slow speeds to allow accurate spraying of

The Adelie penguin, a flightless bird, uses its wings as flippers when it swims.

The ruby-throated hummingbird, which is less than 4 inches (10 cm) long, is one of the smallest birds in North America. It is constantly moving from place to place, eating whenever it has the opportunity.

Although the wild turkey spends most of its time on the ground, it can fly if necessary

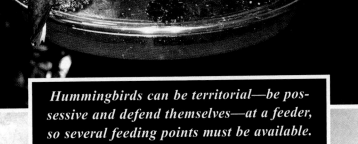

Hummingbirds can be territorial—be possessive and defend themselves—at a feeder, so several feeding points must be available.

The pilot of a hang glider controls the "aircraft" by holding the bottom of the frame and shifting his or her weight in relation to the flexible sail. Once the glider is airborne, it may stay aloft for hours if there are plenty of updrafts.

Some birds, such as these ostriches from Africa, are not designed to fly—they have heavy bones, symmetrical feathers, and a breastbone without a keel.

In March 1999, Bertrand Piccard and Bryan Jones became the first humans to circum-navigate the Earth in a hot-air balloon.

A helicopter is used in rescue operations because of its ability to hover.

The pilot of this experimental V-22 Osprey can change the position of its rotors. When they are horizontal, the aircraft flies like a plane. When they are vertical, it flies like a helicopter.

The Denver International Airport, outside of Denver, Colorado, is about one mile above sea level. At these altitudes, the air is thinner (less dense), which means that airplanes must use more power when taking off.

Precision flying teams, such as the Snowbirds from the Canadian Royal Air Force, can turn in unison, like a flock of geese in a tight formation.

Some of the gliders flown by Otto Lilienthal, the German glider pioneer, resembled bats' wings.

crops. In World War II, single-winged aircraft replaced them. Triplanes, which have three sets of wings on top of one another, were also used in World War I but are rarely seen today.

Cayley also built the first successful full-sized, manned gliders. But it was the German engineer and test pilot Otto Lilienthal who helped perfect the science of human gliding. In his experiments and writings, he presented the secrets of glider control. After making more than 2,000 glider flights, he died in a glider accident in 1896—before he could attach an engine to his glider and attempt powered flight. Lilienthal's books and photographs made people think that human flight was a realistic possibility.

At the time of Lilienthal's death, the American engineer Octave Chanute was also conducting glider experiments. When he began his research, he was in his sixties, and he never conducted test flights of his aircraft. However, he wrote numerous books and articles and encouraged other aviation pioneers in their work. His detailed studies of aviation history were his major contribution to flight research. In fact, Wilbur and Orville Wright were so impressed by Chanute's book, *Progress in Flying Machines,* that they wrote to him. Chanute encouraged the young men to continue their work despite numerous setbacks, and he supported them in their aviation work.

More recently, people have used the principles of gliding to design steerable parachutes. While hanging from these parachutes, skilled sky-divers and military paratroopers can select their desired landing point and if weather conditions permit, they can control their descent and land close to their target. Hang gliders, sailplanes, and military gliders, patterned after the flight of large-winged birds, allow people to fly like condors. Once these aircraft are airborne, they can stay aloft by "riding the thermals" for hours.

Powered Flight

Lack of a lightweight engine was the major problem in the development of powered flight. At the end of the 1890s, steam was industry's primary source of energy. The steam engine had replaced horses, and electricity was being used for more than just household lighting. Motor vehicles that used steam or electric engines were being built. Gasoline engines, still in the development stages, were not reliable.

Gasoline Power

Samuel Langley, an American engineer at the Smithsonian Institution, conducted many experiments with gliders. In the process, he found that steam could be a reliable power source. With an attached steam engine, his model glider flew successfully for ³/₄ of a mile (1.2 km).

Samuel Langley's Aerodrome *crashed after being launched from a houseboat. The assembled newspaper reporters spread news of the failure, which ended Langley's hopes of flight.*

With the support of the U.S. government, Langley decided to try using an internal combustion engine to power a full-size glider. Charles Manley built the engine of the *Aerodrome* and served as its test pilot. In 1903, during each of its two test flights (October 7 and December 8) on a barge in the Potomac River, the *Aerodrome* crashed. The reports of the failure and the withdrawal of government support caused Langley to give up his plans for powered flight.

On December 17, 1903, just nine days after Langley's last failed attempt to achieve powered flight, the Wright brothers flew the *Flyer*, a gasoline-powered biplane. Orville Wright flew the plane over the coastal dunes of Kill Devil Hill, North Carolina. This historic flight, which lasted 12 seconds, covered 120 feet (37 m). That day, the *Flyer* flew three more times, and the longest flight, made by Wilbur Wright, covered 852 feet (260 m). These two brothers had achieved powered, sustained, controlled heavier-than-air flight. Today, the *Flyer* hangs in the Smithsonian National Air and Space Museum, not far from Langley's office.

The Flyer, *designed by Wilbur and Orville Wright, became the first successful heavier-than-air, self-propelled aircraft.*

Jet Power

Because they are both fast and efficient, jet engines are the most common engines used in planes today. The jet engine takes air and compresses it in much the same way that a squid or an octopus uses water. A gas can be compressed more than a liquid, so the force of the released gas is greater. Unlike jet-powered animals, such as squids, jet engines use an internal-combustion engine for power. The fuel is burned in the engine, and the hot gas and outside air are forced through the system. The exhaust rushing backward pushes the plane forward.

Jets first appeared in Germany during World War II (1939–1945), and they were part of the V-1 rocket planes. In 1944, the Germans developed the jet-powered ME-262 rocket, but the war ended before the rockets could be produced in large numbers. Jet-powered aircraft (jets) first saw service in large numbers during the Korean War (1950–1953). In the 1950s, engineers in the United States and Europe developed the modern jet engine for military use.

By 1958, the Boeing Company had begun production of the Boeing 707, the first U.S. passenger jet. In the 1960s, airplane manufacturers began to build commercial aircraft with modern engines. In 1970, the Boeing 747 became the first of many first wide-bodied commercial airliners, which made it possible to carry hundreds of people by air over long distances. A commercial passenger jet can fly at an average speed of about 500 miles (800 km) per hour. That's much faster than a plane with a propeller and a gasoline engine, which can travel at an average speed of about 150 miles (242 km) per hour.

Human Power

Humans have not yet developed a machine that permits us to fly by flapping. The closest we have come is the pedal-powered *Gossamer Condor,* an ultra-light aircraft built by an American named Paul B. MacCready. On August 23, 1977, pilot Bryan Allen flew just over 1 mile (1.6 km) in California to win the Kremer Prize for the first human-powered flight. In 1979, Allen flew the larger *Gossamer Albatross* across the English Channel.

In both flights, a bicyclelike mechanism pedaled by the pilot provided the propulsion. The hips, pelvis, and back allow the legs, with their powerful, thick muscles for long-distance walking, running, and cycling, to act as the engine. Human arms are strong, but the arms, shoulders, and chest

The Gossamer Condor, *the first human-powered aircraft, had a wingspan of 96 feet (29 m). It measured 30 feet (9 m) in length and weighed 70 pounds (32 kg).*

do not have enough muscle to power an aircraft. It is unlikely that we will be able to overcome this limitation, and we will never be able to fly like a bird using flapping flight.

Vertical Flight

Not only can helicopters fly backward, forward, and sideways, but they can take off and land vertically. A helicopter can do all the things a hummingbird can—fly forward, backward, and sideways—and hover. Like the hummingbird, the helicopter can change the angle of attack of its main rotor blades. In helicopters, unlike in hummingbirds, these blades travel in a full circle. Hovering is achieved when the forces of lift and weight are in balance. When this balance changes, the helicopter moves forward, backward, sideways, or up-and-down.

A Short History

Humans had wanted to learn the secrets of vertical flight for centuries, but it took longer to discover how to fly vertically than to fly horizontally. Two scientists who had studied flight in general, Leonardo da Vinci in the fifteenth century, and Sir George Cayley in the nineteenth century, also conducted research into the principles of vertical flight. Both men developed models of aircraft that could fly vertically, but neither built a vertical aircraft that flew successfully.

In an aircraft with rotating blades, each blade is a wing, and as they whirl, they cause the aircraft to rise. The whirling blades, which are airfoils, create lift. In 1907, French inventor Louis Bréguet became the first person to leave the ground—and the first to land safely—in an aircraft powered by spinning blades. Because the aircraft was so difficult to control, four men on the ground had to stabilize it with sticks. On January 9, 1923, Juan de la Cierva, a Spanish aircraft designer, made the first flight in a rotary wing aircraft called the autogyro (or autogiro).

Later, engineers built another smaller type of aircraft, called the gyrocopter. The autogyro and the gyrocopter were similar, but the autogyro was larger and more powerful. Also, the autogyro could take off and land vertically, while the gyrocopter needed a short runway to build up speed. Although both autogyros and gyrocopters couldn't travel far, they gave people an idea of the practical uses of vertical flight. The helicopter has a much greater range.

Engineers in Germany made major improvements in helicopter design and construction. The *Focke-Wulf Fw 61* was one of the first practical helicopters, and the *Focke-Achgels Fa 61* set numerous records, including a cross-country flight of 143 miles (230 km). In 1938, German pilot Hanna Reitsch demonstrated the ability of this helicopter to fly in a small space by flying it inside Deutscheland Halle, a large hall in Berlin. During World War II, Germany manufactured helicopters but did not use them widely.

Autogyros and gyrocopters, which can fly only forward and in circles, cannot hover. Between 1939 and 1940, the American aircraft designer Igor Sikorsky developed and demonstrated a practical design for a modern helicopter. The British and the U.S. armed forces used an improved version of Sikorsky's helicopter in World War II. After World War II, helicopters replaced both autogyros and gyrocopters. The Sikorsky-designed helicopter would eventually serve as the basis for most of the helicopters that now fly throughout the world.

Flight in the Modern Helicopter

A helicopter is governed by Sir Isaac Newton's third law of motion, which states for every action there is an equal and opposite reaction. For example, suppose you are floating near the edge of a swimming pool. If you push off from the side with your hands or your feet, you will move toward the other side, in the opposite direction from the way you pushed.

The same thing happens when a helicopter flies. The force of the blades pushes air downward, which pushes the helicopter upward. The spinning blades create a twisting force, which is known as *torque*. If a helicopter has a single spinning blade, or *rotor*, the *fuselage* rotates in the opposite direction from the blades unless the torque is overcome.

The AH-64 Apache helicopter, manufactured for the U.S. Army, has a tail rotor to balance the torque created by the main rotor. This helicopter can fly at speeds as high as 193 miles (310 km) per hour.

To counteract the torque, a helicopter has a second rotor—usually a tail rotor. The main rotor, the large blade over the fuselage, spins horizontally, and the tail rotor, a small rotor mounted on the tail, rotates vertically. Another name for the tail rotor is the antitorque device, because it counters the rotation of the fuselage and keeps the helicopter steady.

The two rotors move at different speeds, and the ratio between them changes when the pilot flies forward, backward, or sideways. The angle of attack of the blades of the tail rotor can also vary. This is one of the secrets of a helicopter's flexibility. The lifting capacity of the large-diameter rotor allows a helicopter to hover efficiently.

Not every helicopter has a tail rotor to counteract the torque generated by the main rotor. The second rotor may be the same size and turn in the opposite direction, so it cancels out the torque generated by the main rotor. In the tandem arrangement, the two rotors are positioned one behind the other, and in the coaxial arrangement, one rotor is on top of the other.

Chapter 7

Taking Off, Flying, and Landing

For centuries, people studied birds to gain insight into the problems associated with flight. In birds, as well as in insects and bats, the wings are the source of both lift and thrust. In the sophisticated aircraft developed by humans, which are fixed-wing aircraft, the wings provide only lift, while the engines produce the necessary power, or thrust. However, airplanes can be used as simplified models of how animals fly. In both animals and planes, the tail and wings are airfoils.

Airplanes have a variety of *control surfaces* that allow them to fly. On the inside trailing edge of an airplane wing are the *flaps,* and on the outside trailing edge, the *ailerons*. The *rudder,* which is similar to the rudder of a ship, is at a right angle to the fuselage. The *elevators* are the control surfaces on the horizontal tail.

In birds, part of the lift comes from the design of the feathers themselves (see Chapter 3). Unlike an airplane, a bird has only a horizontal tail, a control surface, that helps provide lift. In addition, its tail can act as a rudder and an elevator, to help it move both up and down.

To understand how the different structures work together, the following description of takeoff, actual flight, and landing in airplanes and birds is useful. It takes time and plenty of experience and practice for both animal and human aviators to learn to fly properly.

Leaving the Ground

Takeoff in Airplanes

Before taking off, a pilot must maneuver an airplane into position on the runway, which must be long enough to allow the plane to gather enough speed to leave the ground. This speed is determined by the weight of the plane, the amount of lift the wings can provide, and the local altitude. At high altitudes, air is less dense, and it provides less lift. In the mountains, a plane must either carry a reduced load or use a longer runway to become airborne.

The pilot begins the takeoff by opening the throttle of the engine while pressing on the brakes. (The more the throttle is "opened," the faster the engine runs. To slow the engine, the aircraft is "throttled back.") During this process, which is called a run-up, the pilot checks to see if all the control surfaces—the ailerons, flaps, elevator, and rudder—move freely. The run-up has two purposes. It reduces the amount of runway needed for takeoff by increasing the speed of the air passing under the wings, thus creating lift. It also tests the engine. If the engine behaves in an unexpected way, the pilot aborts, or ends, the takeoff.

If the run-up is successful, the pilot releases the brakes, and the plane rolls forward. When takeoff speed is reached, the pilot pulls back gently on the control wheel and the plane lifts off the ground. The plane climbs under full power. The speed of the air moving over the wings and the shape of the airfoils create lift. Because the plane cannot flap its wings, it is dependent on the engine to provide enough thrust to pull it through the air.

As the plane gains altitude, the pilot retracts the flaps. Why? Consider the shape of an airplane wing when you look along it from its tip toward the fuselage—it's curved. When the wing flaps are lowered, they produce lift by increasing the curvature of the wings. When the flaps are retracted, they reduce lift. The plane's speed increases because the wing is flattened—which makes it more aerodynamic. The amount of curve in the wing caused by the flap being put down from the wings surface increases the amount of lift the wing produces. The plane flies more slowly because the wing is less aerodynamic.

Takeoff in Birds

Birds, like airplanes, take off under full power. However, birds can flap their wings to gain altitude and speed. By adjusting the position of their primary feathers in a downward as well as backward position, they can increase the curvature of their wings. Under normal conditions, birds move only the outer half of their wings during takeoff, using the primary feathers to obtain lift. However, in very difficult conditions, birds flap their entire wings, using their secondary feathers too.

For example, supposing a ground-based enemy, such as a dog, makes a pigeon feel threatened. The bird jumps into the air, flapping its wings hard to gain altitude fast. In the shortest distance possible, it tries to

Like many other birds, the laughing gull needs to run in order to get off the ground.

achieve the height necessary to clear any building or tree in its path. The pigeon must not climb so fast that its wings fail to create lift—it will stall if the angle of attack is too steep. Once the bird is beyond the dog's reach, it will adjust its flight to get to a safer place as quickly as possible.

Birds may leave the ground in other ways, depending on the individual species and the local conditions. Small perching birds, such as sparrows, and birds that roost on cliffs, such as swallows, jump from their perches and use the speed of their dive to become airborne. Larger birds, such as hawks, take off by heading into a strong wind and holding out their wings. A stiff breeze can be enough to lift a bird off the ground.

A bird taking off from water, such as a swan, faces into the wind and runs along the surface until it gets up enough speed to lift off. If there is no wind, the bird reaches as far forward with its wings as possible while running. The forward-and-back movement creates lift by pushing air against the surface of the water.

In the Air

You sometimes hear of airplanes that go out of control and crash. But have you ever seen a bird fall out of the sky? Control of flight usually doesn't pose problems for birds and other animal aviators, because unlike airplanes, they can change the shape of their wings at will—pull them back, spread them out, or change their curvature. By flexing their muscles and making adjustments, birds can prevent stalls that would otherwise cause them to lose control.

What Altitude Is Best?

When an airplane becomes airborne, it ascends from the takeoff point to the desired altitude. It must climb steeply enough to clear any obstacles—but not so steeply that turbulence forms over the wings, because this turbulence decreases lift and may lead to a stall. Sometimes the pilot of a private airplane must follow the directions of an air traffic controller, who requests that the plane fly at a certain altitude. In general, the pilot flies at an altitude that is high enough to avoid obstacles, such as tall towers and buildings, but low enough to avoid commercial airplanes. This altitude is often the level at which the wind increases the speed of the plane.

To climb, the pilot pulls back the control stick. This movement raises the elevator and causes the plane to climb. To descend, the pilot pushes the stick forward and lowers the elevator. Moving the elevator down makes the plane dive. In small planes, a dive is not a normal air maneuver. Unless it is done in an emergency, a dive is generally used by stunt pilots and military fliers. In both cases the pilot has to have extensive training to be able to pull out of a dive at the right time and avoid a crash.

Animals that obtain their food on the wing, such as birds that feed on flying insects, fly at whatever altitude is necessary to catch their prey. A pigeon climbs by pulling its tail under it slightly and increasing its wing beats. A descending pigeon moves its tail up and decreases its wing beats. Migrating birds may fly at high altitudes, but birds that are simply moving around their territory may keep closer to the ground. Birds of prey, such as eagles and hawks, have excellent vision, and they fly high so that they can scan the maximum area with their high-resolution eyesight.

Some birds and bats dive to catch prey. They will usually come in behind and above their quarry and make a steep-angle dive to accelerate and take the prey unaware. Falcons are champions at diving from high altitudes. They position themselves above their prey and may fold their wings. Using a controlled fall, they swoop down in a maneuver that is sometimes called a stoop. A peregrine falcon can stoop at speeds of over 200 miles (320 km) per hour.

Changing Direction

Flying animals and aircraft can move in all three dimensions: up, down, and sideways. When you are standing on the ground, you can move vertically only by jumping. Climbing a steep slope takes a lot of energy, and, of course, you are still on the ground. Skydivers cannot increase their altitude—they can only go down.

Consider that an imaginary rod runs through an animal or an aircraft. A longitudinal axis runs horizontally from front to back. An airplane that is rotating on its longitudinal axis is *rolling*. A lateral axis also runs horizontally but from one wing tip to the other. An airplane that is rotating on its lateral axis is *pitching*. A vertical axis runs through the middle point. An airplane that is rotating on its vertical axis is *yawing*.

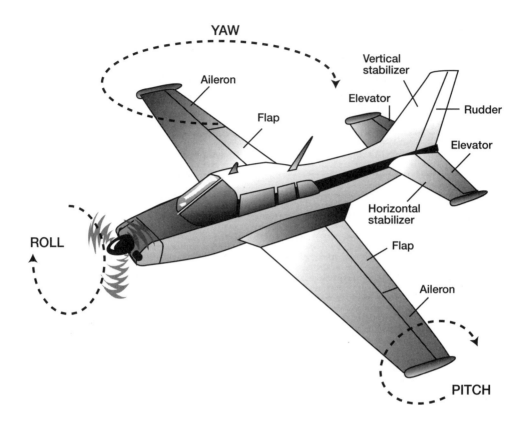

In an airplane, three different rotational motions are possible—around three different axes. Movement about the longitudinal axis, which runs from the nose to the tail, is rolling; movement about the lateral axis, which runs from one wing tip to the other, is pitching; and movement about the vertical axis, which runs in the middle of the plane from the top to the bottom, is yawing.

For example, suppose you are floating face-up in a swimming pool in a few feet of water—with your arms extended, level with your shoulders. To touch the bottom of the pool, you have to turn on your longitudinal axis, or roll. In an aircraft, the ailerons cause the plane to roll. To perform a left roll, the pilot moves the control wheel to the left, which causes the left aileron to rise and the right aileron to lower. To initiate the same maneuver— perform a left roll—a bird uses its primary feathers, moving its left primary feathers down and the right primary feathers up to roll left. The opposite motions on the part of airplane pilots and birds result in a right roll.

Suppose you stopped floating on the water and dived beneath the surface. Then you would be pitching. The pilot of an airplane controls up-and-down motions by moving the elevator on the tail of an aircraft.

But suppose the sun is shining in your eyes so badly that it hurts. Although you still want to face the sky, you want to avoid looking at the bright sun. If you turn left or right but stay on the surface of the water, you are yawing. In order to make a turn in an airplane, the pilot pushes the left rudder pedal to go right, or the right pedal to go left.

To make a graceful turn, the pilot would also lower the right wing so that the plane dipped to the right. This is called a banked turn. To help make the turn smooth, the pilot raises the right aileron and lowers the left one. The skill of the animal or pilot determines how smoothly changes are made.

When a bird wants to turn to the right, it drops its right wing and moves its tail to the left. A bird does not have a rudder. Its tail does the job of both the elevator and rudder. Watch a pigeon flying, and see how it moves its tail when it changes direction.

Landing: The Hardest Part

Two sayings—"flying is optional, landing is not" and "the number of landings must equal the number of takeoffs"—are a good indicator of the importance of a smooth return to Earth. Landing is more complicated than taking off because airfoils are made to keep the plane or animal airborne. The aerodynamic nature of the wings must be overcome to ensure a proper return to Earth.

Landing a plane requires the pilot to maintain a precise angle of descent called the glide path. (The word "gliding" refers to the plane's not using power to maintain altitude.) The pilot uses the glide path to ensure that the plane does not meet the runway so near the end that the plane does not have enough room to stop. There is also a danger of descending too steeply and missing the beginning of the runway.

A plane must reduce forward speed quickly as it approaches its landing site. With the decrease in speed, lift is lost. The pilot then brings the nose up, which increases the angle of attack and generates additional lift. To increase the lift still further, the pilot gradually lowers the flaps in stages as the plane makes its approach. The purpose is to slow the plane

Making Landing an Airplane Easier

To help pilots find the proper glide path, runways at airports in the United States and Canada have markings that allow pilots to maintain their glide path by using a certain combination of colored markers. There are two rows of lights, white and red. Only when a pilot is on the correct glide path do the markers appear in a certain combination—the red lights appear above the white lights.

as much as possible while the plane gently descends and lands. When these procedures are done correctly, the plane stalls—and loses lift completely—just as the wheels touch down.

A small propeller plane runs a short distance along the runway to lose the remainder of its forward speed before the pilot applies the brakes to bring it to a stop. However, a jet is so powerful that the pilot must reverse its engines before applying the brakes.

The pilot who is landing a jet on an aircraft carrier has no margin for error. To become qualified to land planes on an aircraft carrier, a military pilot must have hundreds of hours of flying time and have landed planes successfully on a 700-foot (213-m) practice runway. The 1,000-foot (304-m) runway doesn't give the pilot enough room to use the brakes to slow down, so four sets of arresting cables are spread across the deck to stop planes. Planes have a hook under the tail to snag the wire.

A bird uses a slightly different procedure to land. The animal slows its forward speed and changes its body position from horizontal to vertical, thus increasing its angle of attack The animal then spreads its tail to act as a brake, and it does a backstroke with its wings to reduce its airspeed. If the wind is blowing, the animal tries to land into the wind so that its tail and wings produce maximum air resistance. When a bird lands, it pulls its tail into its original position only when its feet are about to touch the ground.

A bird chooses its glide path depending on specific conditions. A tern landing in a crowded colony may make a nearly vertical landing. A swan

Large birds, such as the mute swan, need plenty of room to land. The swan uses its feet as brakes when it lands on the water.

coming into a lake may make a long approach, then flip its wings vertically to slow down and just let its feet skid across the water until it stops. A bird landing on a rocky ledge must come to a standstill while still in midair and then put its feet down. The same is true for bats landing at a roost. Sometimes they even land upside down!

When you watch a bird preparing to land, consider all the factors the animal must control to make a good landing. Although it may take years for a person to learn to fly a plane safely, it may take only a few weeks for a bird to master the air. For a "bird brain," that's quite a feat!

We Still Have a Lot to Learn

Millions of years ago, before humans appeared on Earth, animals developed ways to move through the air. Insects developed the ability to fly even before dinosaurs appeared. Birds flew before dinosaurs became extinct. Bats became fliers more recently (but still millions of years ago).

The Daedalus-Icarus story in Greek mythology is only one expression of the human dream of flight. As scientific study progressed, people began to study nature's aviators with the hope of learning their secrets. Technological advances in aviation, such as the modern jetliner, allow people to fly from one end of the world to the other in just a few hours. For example, a jetliner now takes about 8 hours to fly between New York and London. A supersonic jet, such as the Concorde, which can travel faster than the speed of sound, takes a little more than 3 hours to fly the same distance.

In addition, in the last 100 years, people have learned a tremendous amount about outer space. This knowledge has allowed humans to take trips to the moon and return safely, and send unmanned spacecraft to other planets.

But with all this advanced science and technology, we still do not have a comprehensive theory that explains how birds can fly the length of two continents and return to the same place a year later. And we don't know how honeybees fly or how bats find their way to a roosting site hundreds of miles away. Some forms of animal aviation still present mysteries.

Glossary

aerodynamics—the science that deals with air and other gaseous fluids and how they react with objects such as animals or aircraft moving through them

ailerons—flaps on the outer trailing edges of airplane wings, which help turn the aircraft

airfoil—a structure designed to produce lift

air speed—the speed of an aircraft relative to the air

altitude—the elevation of an object

alula—the feathers on the front (leading) edge of a bird's wing

angle of attack—the angle of the wing of an animal or aircraft relative to the direction of flight

beam wind—a wind coming from the side

Bernoulli's principle—a principle stating that the increase in the speed of flow of a fluid results in a decrease in pressure

blimp—a lighter-than-air aircraft that uses internal gas bags for lift. It does not have a rigid internal framework.

control surface—any part of a flying animal or aircraft whose shaped can be changed to affect the way the animal or aircraft flies. The wings, feathers, and tail of a bird are control surfaces, and the wings, ailerons, flaps, rudder, and tail of an airplane are control surfaces.

contour feather—a medium-sized feather that determines the shape of a bird

density—the amount of material per unit volume

dirigible—a lighter-than-air aircraft that can be steered. Airships with rigid internal frameworks are dirigibles. ·

drag—a force caused by the friction of air against a moving body

echolocation—the process of using reflections of sound waves to locate objects

elevator—a control surface on the horizontal tail of an airplane that raises or lowers the plane's nose

flaps—control surfaces on the inside of the trailing edge of the wings of an airplane. Flaps increase the surface area of the wing when they are lowered during takeoff and landing.

fossil—the preserved remains of a plant or an animal

fossil record—fossils found in geologic formations that provide a picture of the history of life on Earth. Paleontologists are scientists who study the fossil record.

fuselage—the body of an airplane or helicopter

gliding—a controlled fall; a type of unpowered flight

ground speed—the speed of an aircraft with relation to the ground

head wind—a wind coming from the front

hover—to remain suspended over one place

keel-shaped—resembling the shape of the long piece of wood along the bottom of a boat

lift—the force that overcomes gravity and allows an animal or aircraft to rise

migration—the seasonal movement from place to place usually associated with moving to and from breeding sites

pitch—movement up or down from the horizontal

powered flight—flying that uses energy

predator—an animal that hunts other animals for food

pressure—force per unit of area (coming from all sides)

pterosaur—an extinct order of flying reptiles that lived during the Mesozoic Era (230 to 65 million years ago)

relative wind—the wind created by a moving object

roll—to spin, as in an airplane

roost—(verb) to settle down for rest or sleep; (noun) a place where birds or bats rest or sleep

rotor—the blades of a helicopter. Most helicopters have a main rotor over the fuselage that rotates horizontally and a tail rotor at the rear that rotates vertically.

rudder—control surface on the vertical part of a plane's tail that contributes to steering

shaft—the center axis of a feather

soaring—a type of gliding that involves the use of true wings. Animals and craft that can soar are able to move upward on air currents and downward in response to gravity.

stall—the loss of lift around an airfoil

streamline—to have a smooth outline that allows air to take the shortest path from one point to another

tail wind—a wind coming from behind

thrust—the force that propels animals or aircraft through the air

torque—a turning or twisting force

turbulence—rough, irregular movement of air

unpowered flight—flying that involves no expenditure of energy. Gliding and soaring are two types of unpowered flight.

velocity—speed of movement

weight—total mass under normal gravity

yaw—side-to-side movement

End Notes

Chapter 1

1. Thor Heyerdahl, *Kon-Tiki.* (New York: Washington Square Press, 1950).

Chapter 3

1. Kate Douglas Wiggen and Nora A. Smith, *The Arabian Nights: Their Best-Known Tales.* (New York: Barnes & Noble Books, 1993), 298–299.

Chapter 4

1. P. Weiss, "The buzz: wings flip, air whirls, bugs lift," *Science News,* 19 June 1999, 390. (Report of "Wing Rotation and the Aerodynamic Basis of Insect Flight," Michael H. Dickinson, Sanjay P. Sane, and Fritz-Olaf Lehmann, *Science News,* 18 June 1999.)

Chapter 6

1. Civil Air Patrol, *Your Aerospace World.* (Alabama: Maxwell Air Force Base). (No date of publication given.)

Projects You Can Do

One advantage of doing a science project is that you can investigate an idea that interests you. The only things that limit your research are time, money, and imagination—the same things that limit all scientists. *Bernoulli's Book* has 25 experiments on aerodynamics. *Science Fair Survival Techniques for Kids, Parents, and Teachers* is a good general reference on projects for science fairs; its "Plan of Action" section tells you how to get started. See the To Find Out More section for more information about the following books and any others that might prove helpful.

A Wind Tunnel
(basic design from *Scientific American Frontiers*, Teaching Guide for Show #904 [2000])

Once you have set up this apparatus, there is no end to the kinds of experiments you can do. For example, you can fold paper airplanes in different ways and place them in the wind tunnel to see which ones result in better airflow.

1. Place a table that is a minimum of 3.3 feet (1 m) long and approximately waist high against a wall.
2. Attach a grid of 1.6-inch (4-cm) squares to the wall. The grid should be at least 24 inches high by 35 inches wide (60 by 90-cm).
3. Place a three-speed box fan at one end of the table so that the "wind" blows along the table. The height of the fan can be adjusted by raising the fan on stacks of books or boxes.
4. Attach models of various types of planes to sticks so that they can stand in the wind tunnel when the fan is on. The planes can also be attached to a separate stick that can then be adjusted on the upright. In this way the angle of the plane in relation to the ground can be changed. Make sure the base is stable or held down with weights or books.
5. Make the "wind" visible by having a bowl with theatrical smoke (or dry ice) above the fan. The dry-ice vapor will sink, and as it passes the fan, the airstream over the wings of the model will become visible.
6. A video camera should be positioned at a right angle to the plane being tested. This allows it to record the airstream as it passes over the wings.
7. Once you have tested your planes at various speeds and completed videotaping, review the tape at normal speed and then at slow speed. See which planes have the least turbulence at various angles of attack.

Insect Wings and the Strength of Pleats

An insect's wing is even stronger per unit of its weight than the paper you will use in this experiment—it is reinforced with veins.

1. Take a flat sheet of paper and hold it vertically by one edge. Place a weight made of two or three washers on the top edge where you are holding it. What happens?
2. Put the paper on the edge of a table. Anchor one end with a book and let the other end hang off the table. Put the weight on the paper's surface beyond the edge of the table. Again, what happens?
3. Now fold the paper into at least six pleats so that it looks a bit like an accordion. Stand the paper upright so that it forms a column. Place a piece of cardboard on the top of the column and then put the washers on top of the cardboard.
4. Put the paper on the table in the same way as in step 1. Place cardboard on top with the washers and see how it can hold them up. By folding another piece of paper with more pleats, the paper can hold more weight.
5. Pinch the base of the folded paper to form a fan. How many washers can the paper fan hold?

A Water-Bottle Rocket

Water-bottle rockets will give you a simple demonstration of a jet powered by compressed air and water under pressure. The activity outlined below is the simplest of the things you can do with water-bottle rockets. This Science Fair project can be found in *Bernoulli's Book* (see the To Find Out More section for more information). Water-bottle rockets are used in Japan to carry rescue lines across ravines and small rivers. These are more sophisticated than the one outlined here, but the principle is the same. Be sure to build this rocket outdoors.

1. Obtain a 2-liter soft drink bottle (with its cap), some hose (such as a big plastic hose from an aquarium), and a bicycle pump. Using a knife, make a hole in the cap, large enough to fit the hose into the bottle.
2. Fill the bottle with water so it is one-third full. Screw the cap on.
3. Attach the bicycle pump to the end of the hose. Turn the bottle upside down, and hold it up-right with any suitable objects, such as rocks. Pump the bicycle pump until the rocket takes off.

To Find Out More

Other useful materials besides these books, computer programs, and videotapes are available. Check with your public library to obtain new information or learn more about a particular subject.

Basic Books and Articles

Ackerman, Jennifer. "Dinosaurs Take Wing." *National Geographic*. July, 1998.

Agency for Instructional Technology. *What Goes Up*. Cincinnati, OH: South-Western Educational Publishing, 1998.

Baker, Robin (editor). *The Mystery of Migration*. New York: Viking Press (Studio Books), 1981.

Bodsworth, Fred. *The Last of the Curlews*. Richmond Hill, Ontario, Canada: Scholastic-TAB Publications, 1985.

Civil Air Patrol. *Your Aerospace World*. Alabama: Maxwell Air Force Base. (No date of publication given.)

Hixson, B.K. *Bernoulli's Book*. Salt Lake City, UT: Wild Goose Company, 1991.

Long, Robert A., and Samuel P. Welles. *All New Dinosaurs and Their Friends from the Great Recent Fossil Discoveries*. Santa Barbara, CA: Bellerophon Books, 1984.

Science Fair Survival Techniques for Kids, Parents, and Teachers. Salt Lake City, UT: Wild Goose Company, 1997.

Smithsonian Migratory Bird Center. *Feathered Travelers*. Washington, DC: Smithsonian Institution Press. (No date of publication given.)

Taylor, Kim. *Flying Start Science: Flight*. North Billerica, MA: Curriculum Associates, 1992.

Tekulsky, Mathew. *The Hummingbird Garden*. New York: Crown Publishers, 1990.

Wilson, Don E. *Bats in Question: The Smithsonian Answer Book*. Washington, DC: Smithsonian Institution Press, 1997.

Xerces Society and the Smithsonian Institution. *Butterfly Gardening*. Washington, DC: Sierra Club Books and the National Wildlife Federation, 1990.

More Specialized Books and Articles

Brackenbury, John. *Insects in Flight*. London, England: Blandford Books, 1992.

Burton, Robert. *Bird Flight*. New York: Facts on File, 1990.

Chatterjee, Sankar. *The Rise of Birds*. Baltimore, MD: Johns Hopkins University Press, 1997.

Gollop, J.B., T.W. Barry, and E.H. Iversen. *Eskimo Curlew: A Vanishing Species?* Regina, Saskatchewan, Canada: Saskatchewan Natural History Society, 1986.

Graham, Joe M. (editor). *The Hive and the Honey Bee*. Hamilton, IL: Dadant and Sons, 1992.

Levi, Wendell Mitchell. *The Pigeon*. Sumter, SC: Levi Publishing Company, 1986.

Padian, Kevin. "The Origin and Aerodynamics of Pterosaurs." *Paleobiology* (Volume 28, Number 3), 1985.

Pettingill, Olin Sewall. *Ornithology in Laboratory and Field* (5th ed.) New York: Academic Press, 1985.

Shipman, Pat. *Taking Wing:* Archaeopteryx *and the Evolution of Bird Flight*. New York: Simon & Schuster, 1998.

Urquhart, Fred A. *The Monarch Butterfly: International Traveler*. Chicago: Nelson-Hall, 1987.

Vaughan, Terry A. *Mammalogy* (3rd ed.) New York: Saunders College Publishing, 1986.

Wilson, Mary F. *Vertebrate Natural History*. New York: Saunders College Publishing, 1984.

Instruction Kit

"Mystery of the First Feathered Flight." Bellingham, WA: Creative Dimensions. (No publication date given.)

Computer Programs

The Discovery Channel and Marris, "How Animals Move," 1995 (CD-ROM).

National Aeronautics and Space Administration (NASA). "FoilSim," 1997 (disk).

Videos

"Flight" (Eyewitness Series). New York: DK Vision. (No date of production given.)

"Water Rocket Series" (volumes 1–3). Pittsburg, KS: Pitsco Inc. (No date of production given.)

Organizations and Online Sites

Use the Internet or other research facilities to determine what new discoveries relating to animal flight have been made and how they relate to older material. To find out more about mechanized flight, contact clubs about building and flying model aircraft and model rockets.

Aerospace Education

Aerospace Education Foundation
1501 Lee Highway
Arlington, VA 22209
http://www.aef.org
A national organization that promotes aeronautical and aerospace education.

Aircraft Owners and Pilots Association
421 Aviation Way
Frederick, MD 21701
http://www.aopa.org
A national organization of private pilots that provides information on flying and aircraft ownership.

American Helicopter Society—
Vertical Flight Society
217 North Washington Street
Alexandria, VA 22314
http://www.vtol.org
A national organization of helicopter
pilots that provides information on
rotorcraft flying and ownership.

American Institute of Aeronautics
and Astronautics
1801 Alexander Bell Drive, Suite 500
Reston, VA 20191
http://www.aiaa.org
A national organization that promotes
aeronautical and aerospace education.

Civil Air Patrol
105 South Hansell Street
Maxwell Air Force Base, AL 36112
http://www.capnhg.gov
A United States Air Force Auxiliary that
provides aeronautical and aerospace
education, leadership training, and
conducts search and rescue operations.

Federal Aviation Administration
800 Independence Avenue, S.W.
Washington, DC 20591
http://www.faa.gov
A federal agency that regulates almost all
aspects of civilian aviation.

National Aeronautics and
Space Administration
Education Division, Mail Code FE
Washington, DC 20546
http://education.nasa.gov
A federal agency that conducts
research in aeronautics and aerospace.
It also promotes aeronautical and
aerospace education.

Soaring Society of America
P.O. Box 2100
Hobbs, NM 88241
http://www.ssa.org
A national organization of glider and
sailplane owners that provides information on flying and aircraft ownership.

Conservation

American Bird Conservancy
1250 24th Street N.W., Suite 220
Washington, DC 20037
http://www.abcbirds.org
A conservation organization that
promotes bird conservation and
environmental education.

Bat Conservation International
P.O. Box 162603
Austin, TX 78716
http://www.batcon.org
A national organization that promotes bat
conservation and bat-related research.

Birdlife International
Wellbrook Court, Girton Road
Cambridge CB3 0NA
United Kingdom
http://www.wing-wbsj.or.jp/birdlife/
A global alliance of bird conservation
organizations.

Cornell Laboratory of Ornithology
159 Sapsucker Woods Road
Ithaca, NY 14850
http://www.ornith.cornell.edu
An organization devoted to interpreting
and conserving bird diversity through
research, educational programs, and
public programs focused on birds.

Monarch Watch
Department of Entomology
Haworth Hall
University of Kansas
Lawrence, KS 66045
http://www.monarchwatch.org
An organization that promotes environmental education through hands-on butterfly biology programs and participation in online investigations of monarch butterfly migration. Monarch Watch provides information about the behavior of caterpillars and butterflies, tagging programs, and other topics.

National Audubon Society
700 Broadway
New York, NY 10003
http://www.audubon.org
A national conservation organization that focuses on preserving natural ecosystems through various means, including environmental education.

National Wildlife Federation
8925 Leesburg Pike
Vienna, VA 22184
http://www.nwf.org
An organization that focuses on conserving wildlife and other natural resources by increasing environmental awareness in people of all ages.

Smithsonian Migratory Bird Center
National Zoological Park
Washington, DC 20008
http://web2.si.edu/smbc
A national bird conservation organization dedicated to understanding bird migration through research and education.

The Xerces Society
4828 Southeast Hawthorne Boulevard
Portland, OR 97215
http://www.xerces.org
An organization focused on public education about invertebrates, including butterflies, and their conservation.

Index

111

About The Author

Eve Iversen, an ornithologist with two master's degrees, has published more than 30 scientific reports and has helped write three books, including *Eskimo Curlew: A Vanishing Species?* In 1998, she trained at the National Space Biomedical Research Institute program at Texas A&M University and the National Aeronautics and Space Administration (NASA), Houston. In 1999, she received a Woodrow Wilson Fellowship to study biodiversity. Recently she received a Fulbright grant to allow her to study in Egypt. She teaches high school science in the San Francisco Bay area, and she lives in northern California.